Common Core Connections
Language Arts
Grade 4

Carson-Dellosa Publishing, LLC
Greensboro, North Carolina

Credits
Content Editor: Christine Schwab
Copy Editor: Elise Craver

Visit *carsondellosa.com* for correlations to Common Core, state, national, and
Canadian provincial standards.

Carson-Dellosa Publishing, LLC
PO Box 35665
Greensboro, NC 27425 USA
carsondellosa.com

ISBN 978-1-62442-795-4

01-244131151

Table of Contents

Introduction

What Are the Common Core State Standards for English Language Arts?

The standards are a shared set of expectations for each grade level in the areas of reading, writing, speaking, listening, and language. They define what students should understand and be able to do. The standards are designed to be more rigorous and allow for students to justify their thinking. They reflect the knowledge that is necessary for success in college and beyond.

As described in the Common Core State Standards, students who master the standards in reading, writing, speaking, listening, and language as they advance through the grades will exhibit the following capabilities:

1. They demonstrate independence.
2. They build strong content knowledge.
3. They respond to the varying demands of audience, task, purpose, and discipline.
4. They comprehend as well as critique.
5. They value evidence.
6. They use technology and digital media strategically and capably.
7. They come to understand other perspectives and cultures.*

How to Use This Book

This book is a collection of practice pages aligned to the Common Core State Standards for English Language Arts and appropriate for fourth grade. Included is a skill matrix so that you can see exactly which standards are addressed on the practice pages. Also included are a skill assessment and a skill assessment analysis. Use the assessment at the beginning of the year or at any time of year you wish to assess your students' mastery of certain standards. The analysis connects each test item to a practice page or set of practice pages so that you can review skills with students who struggle in certain areas.

* © Copyright 2010. National Governors Association Center for Best Practices and Council of Chief State School Officers. All rights reserved.

Common Core State Standards*
Alignment Matrix

Pages	12	13	14	15	16	17	18	19	20	21	22	23	24	25	26	27	28	29	30	31	32	33	34	35	36	37	38	39	40	41	42	43	44	45	46	47	48	49	50	51
4.RL.1		•	•							•				•																										
4.RL.2	•			•																																				
4.RL.3			•			•	•							•		•																								
4.RL.4								•		•																														
4.RL.5												•																												•
4.RL.6							•									•																								
4.RL.7															•																									
4.RL.9																•																								
4.RL.10	•	•					•	•		•		•		•		•																		•		•				
4.RI.1																	•	•		•	•									•		•		•		•				
4.RI.2																	•	•	•																	•				
4.RI.3																							•																	
4.RI.4																								•						•				•	•					
4.RI.5																						•	•			•														
4.RI.6																										•														
4.RI.7																						•	•													•				
4.RI.8																			•																					
4.RI.9																												•												
4.RI.10																			•	•	•	•	•	•	•		•	•	•		•			•						
4.RF.3																																					•	•		
4.RF.3a																																					•	•		
4.RF.4																																					•	•	•	•
4.RF.4a																																								
4.RF.4b																																						•		
4.RF.4c																																				•			•
4.W.1																																								
4.W.1a																																								
4.W.1b																																								
4.W.1c																																								
4.W.1d																																								
4.W.2																																								
4.W.2a																																								
4.W.2b																																								
4.W.2c																																								
4.W.2d																																								
4.W.2e																																								
4.W.3			•																																					
4.W.3a																																								
4.W.3b			•																																					
4.W.3c																																								
4.W.3d			•																																					
4.W.3e			•																																					
4.W.4																										•														
4.W.5																										•														
4.W.6																										•														
4.W.7																										•														
4.W.8																																								
4.W.9																																								
4.W.9a																																								
4.W.9b																																								
4.W.10																																								
4.L.1																																								
4.L.1a																																								
4.L.1b																																								
4.L.1c																																								
4.L.1d																																								
4.L.1e																																								
4.L.1f																																								
4.L.1g																																								
4.L.2																																								
4.L.2a																																								
4.L.2b																																								
4.L.2c																																								
4.L.2d																																								
4.L.3																																								
4.L.3a																																								
4.L.3b																																								
4.L.3c																																								
4.L.4								•		•														•										•		•				
4.L.4a								•																•										•						
4.L.4b										•																										•				
4.L.4c																																								
4.L.5																																		•			•			•
4.L.5a																																								•
4.L.5b																																								
4.L.5c																																		•						
4.L.6																																								

Common Core State Standards*
Alignment Matrix

Pages	52	53	54	55	56	57	58	59	60	61	62	63	64	65	66	67	68	69	70	71	72	73	74	75	76	77	78	79	80	81	82	83	84	85	86	87	88	89	90
4.RL.1																																							
4.RL.2																																							
4.RL.3																																							
4.RL.4																																							
4.RL.5																																							
4.RL.6																																							
4.RL.7																																							
4.RL.9																																							
4.RL.10	•																																	•					
4.RI.1																																							
4.RI.2																																							
4.RI.3																																							
4.RI.4																																							
4.RI.5																																							
4.RI.6																																							
4.RI.7																																							
4.RI.8																																							
4.RI.9																																							
4.RI.10			•		•		•																																•
4.RF.3		•		•		•		•																															
4.RF.3a			•			•		•																															
4.RF.4	•		•	•	•	•	•	•																															
4.RF.4a	•		•			•		•																															
4.RF.4b	•				•																																		
4.RF.4c					•		•																																
4.W.1											•	•																											
4.W.1a											•	•																											
4.W.1b											•	•																											
4.W.1c											•																												
4.W.1d												•																											
4.W.2										•													•																
4.W.2a										•																													
4.W.2b										•																													
4.W.2c																							•																
4.W.2d														•	•																								
4.W.2e																							•																
4.W.3									•			•		•		•	•	•				•																	
4.W.3a									•							•	•					•																	
4.W.3b																			•																				
4.W.3c													•																										
4.W.3d														•																									
4.W.3e															•	•																							
4.W.4																		•																					
4.W.5																						•		•															
4.W.6																						•		•															
4.W.7																		•																					
4.W.8													•																										
4.W.9																	•	•																					
4.W.9a																	•																						
4.W.9b																		•																					
4.W.10													•	•					•		•		•																
4.L.1		•																							•	•	•	•											
4.L.1a																						•																	
4.L.1b																										•													
4.L.1c																										•													
4.L.1d																												•											
4.L.1e																												•											
4.L.1f																											•												
4.L.1g																												•											
4.L.2		•																											•	•	•								
4.L.2a																													•	•									
4.L.2b																													•	•									
4.L.2c																													•										
4.L.2d																																•							
4.L.3																																	•	•	•				
4.L.3a																																		•					
4.L.3b																																		•					
4.L.3c																																	•						
4.L.4								•																													•		
4.L.4a																																							
4.L.4b																																							
4.L.4c								•																													•		
4.L.5				•																															•	•	•	•	
4.L.5a																																			•	•	•		
4.L.5b																																				•	•		
4.L.5c				•																																		•	
4.L.6																																							•

© Carson-Dellosa • CD-104611

Read the passage. Then, answer the questions.

The Raven and the Pitcher

For months, rain had failed to fall in the high desert country. The cacti's fleshy leaves, always a source of water for thirsty animals, had dried and withered into flat, leathery discs. Creeks and pools had turned to clay.

A parched raven circled high above in the sky. Weak from thirst, he knew that he could not live long without any water. Spotting something shining in a deserted campsite below, the raven swooped down. It was a glass pitcher half-filled with water! But, when the raven put his beak into the pitcher, he couldn't reach the water.

Now desperate, he thought and thought until he had an idea. Grabbing a small pebble from the ground, he dropped it into the pitcher. Then, he dropped another. He dropped more pebbles into the pitcher. With each pebble, the water rose closer to the top. At last, he was able to **drink his fill** and save his life.

1. In "The Raven and The Pitcher," why was the Raven desperate? How do you know?

_____

2. What is the moral of this story? _____

3. What was Raven's problem? How did he solve it? _____

4. Find a word in the passage that best fits the definition below.

   A. chunky _____   B. thirsty _____

   C. dove _____   D. frantic _____

5. What does the phrase *drink his fill* mean? _____

6. What is this kind of story called? _____

7. How would this story be different if told by a coyote? _____

Circle the word that best completes the sentence.

8. The man was hungry and _____ to find some food.

   sad   desperate   soon

9. She poured a glass of milk from the _____.

   pitcher   picture   pincer

10. What other story have you read about a main character overcoming adversity?

_____

Read the passage. Then, answer the questions.

Night Animals

As you turn off the bedroom light and your parents tuck you in, animals outside your window are starting to wake up. These are **nocturnal** animals. Each of these animals has one sense—touch, sight, smell, taste, or hearing—that is unusually suited to night life.

Humans are **diurnal**, which means they are mostly awake during the day. To study nocturnal animals, you need only a few tools. You'll need a flashlight, a pair of binoculars, a small magnifying glass, a pencil, a pad of paper, and an afternoon nap!

Safety first! Take a parent or another adult with you. Also, wear closed-toe shoes. Ready? Here we go!

11. What is the main idea of the passage? _____

12. What is the difference between *nocturnal* and *diurnal* creatures? _____

13. Roly-polies hide under the edges of lawns during the day. Why do you think they do this?

_____

14. How do nocturnal animals get around in the night since there is no light? Refer to the passage

for the answer. _____

15. Why does the writer suggest you wear closed-toe shoe for this adventure? _____

_____

16. Circle which happens first in a day.

A. people wake up   nocturnal animals wake up

B. nighttime hike   gather hiking tools

C. bats sleep   you sleep

17. Describe how you would react if you came upon an owl in the dark. Compare it with how you

think the owl would react. _____

_____

_____

_____

18. The author suggests two safety rules. Write two more. _____

_____

_____

19. Write an essay about a topic that interests you. The writing can be based on personal experience or research. Be sure your essay includes

- an introduction of the topic;
- facts, definitions, and details relating to the topic;
- words and phrases that link ideas (such as *another, for example, also, because*);
- precise language;
- a conclusion related to the topic.

Write the first draft of your essay below. Read your essay to another person to see if there are any suggestions. Then, rewrite your final draft on another sheet of paper or on the computer.

_____

_____

_____

_____

_____

_____

_____

_____

_____

_____

_____

_____

_____

_____

_____

_____

_____

_____

_____

Circle the correct words.

20. Jose is the boy (who whom whose) I ride (too to two) school with.

Rewrite the sentence using correct capitalization, punctuation, and spelling.

21. i went to the yard sail but i didn't by anything Tasha said

_____

22. Write two sentences about a boy and a dog. The first sentence should tell facts. The second sentence should show excitement. _____

_____

Circle the definition that best explains the underlined word.

23. The outer coverings of many creepy <u>crawlies</u> look crunchy and hard.

   A. a kind of crayfish

   B. a creature that crawls

   C. a mother bird

24. The suffix –*est* means the most. Add it to each of these words. Then, write the meaning.

   A. dark_____ means _____

   B. sweet_____ means _____

   C. soft_____ means _____

   D. light_____ means _____

Underline the simile or metaphor in each sentence. Then, write its meaning.

25. After the game, Ted felt like a limp dishrag. _____

26. The race car hogged the road. _____

27. Tell what this idiom means: Two wrongs don't make a right. _____

_____

28. Circle the synonym of *swift*.

   slow   tasty   rapid

29. Circle the antonym of *moist*.

   wet   sticky   dry

30. Circle the vocabulary words most likely to be found in an essay about snakes.

   sweet   slithering   reptile   honest   fangs   scales   happy

After you score each student's skill assessment pages, match any incorrectly answered problems to the table below. Use the corresponding practice pages for any problem areas and ensure that each student receives remediation in these areas.

Answer Key: 1. Raven saw water, but couldn't get to it. 2. Some of the hardest problems are solved a little at a time. 3. Raven couldn't get his beak down to the water, so he raised the water level with pebbles. 4. A. fleshy; B. parched; C. swooped; D. desperate; 5. drank as much as he needed; 6. fable; 7. Answers will vary, but should emphasize the difference between having wings or four legs in this situation. 8. desperate; 9. pitcher; 10. Answers will vary. 11. Many animals wake up at night. 12. Nocturnal animals are awake at night. Diurnal creatures are awake during the day. 13. Answers will vary, but should have to do with them being nocturnal. 14. They use one of their other senses. 15. because you could easily bump your toes on something you can't see in the dark; 16. A. people wake up; B. gather hiking tools; C. you sleep; 17. Answers will vary. 18. Answers will vary. 19. Essays will vary. 20. whom, to; 21. "I went to the yard sale, but I didn't buy anything," Tasha said. 22. Answers will vary but the first sentence should end in a period, the second with an exclamation mark; 23. B; 24. A. darkest, the most dark; B. sweetest, the most sweet; C. softest, the most soft; D. lightest, the most light; 25. like a limp dishrag, tired; 26. hogged, took up the whole road; 27. Answers will vary. 28. rapid; 29. dry; 30. slithering, reptile, fangs, scales

Common Core State Standards*		Test Item(s)	Practice Page(s)
Reading Standards for Literature			
Key Ideas and Details	4.RL.1 – 4.RL.3	1–3	12–17, 21, 25, 27, 28
Craft and Structure	4.RL.4 – 4.RL.6	4–9	18, 19, 21, 23, 27, 51, 53
Integration of Knowledge and Ideas	4.RL.9	10	27
Range of Reading and Level of Text Complexity	4.RL.10	1–7	12, 13, 17, 18, 20, 22, 24, 25, 26, 42, 44, 52
Reading Standards for Informational Text			
Key Ideas and Details	4.RI.1 – 4.RI.3	11, 13, 14, 18	29–32, 41, 43, 45, 47
Craft and Structure	4.RI.4 – 4.RI.6	12, 17, 19	33–35, 37, 38, 41, 45, 47
Integration of Knowledge and Ideas	4.RI.8	15, 16, 20	29, 33, 34
Range of Reading and Level of Text Complexity	4.RI.10	11–18	30–36, 39, 40, 42, 44, 46, 54, 56, 58
Reading Standards: Foundational Skills			
Phonics and Word Recognition	4.RF.3	4, 8, 9	48, 49, 53, 55, 57, 59
Fluency	4.RF.4	1–3, 5–7, 10	49–52, 54, 55–59
Writing			
Text Types and Purposes	4.W.1 – 4.W.3	19	14, 62–64, 66–68, 72, 74
Production and Distribution of Writing	4.W.4 – 4.W.6	19	37, 61, 71, 73, 75
Research to Build and Present Knowledge	4.W.7 – 4.W.9	19	65, 69, 70
Language			
Conventions of Standard English	4.L.1 – 4.L.2	20, 21	23, 76–82
Knowledge of Language	4.L.3	22	60, 83, 84
Vocabulary Acquisition and Use	4.L.4 – 4.L.6	23–30	19, 35, 43, 48, 51, 55, 59, 85–90

* © Copyright 2010. National Governors Association Center for Best Practices and Council of Chief State School Officers. All rights reserved.

Write the letter for the main idea of each paragraph.

_____ 1.   Gary and Fritz had been writing to each other for four years. Gary lived in Indiana, and Fritz lived in West Germany. Gary looked forward to Fritz's letters. Fritz usually sent at least one picture, and sometimes, he sent extra German stamps for Gary's collection. Gary and Fritz both hope that they can meet someday. They feel as if they know each other already.

     A. pictures from Germany
     B. Gary's German pen pal
     C. Gary's friend

_____ 2.   Mary has been blind all of her life. She has gone to special schools to learn how to do things for herself. Her best friend Katy is not blind. Mary and Katy help each other. Mary is trying to teach Katy to read braille. It is a special system of raised dots that lets Mary read the page. Katy is not doing very well at all. Katy says that it is hard for her to "see" the letters with her fingers.

     A. learning to read
     B. problems of being blind
     C. a special friendship

_____ 3.   It is September. it is the night of the first football game of the year. Everyone at Kidwell School is excited. Most excited of all is Cliff. This is the very first night that he has ever marched with the band. He holds his clarinet nervously. As the director's white glove raises up, Cliff's heart skips a beat. He has dreamed of this moment, and it is finally here. He is a member of the marching band at last!

     A. Cliff's first night as a band member
     B. excitement on the night of the first game
     C. Cliff and his friends at the football game

_____ 4.   There were so many different frames. Some were very large, and some were very small. Some were simple, and some were fancy. Carol liked every pair she tried on. Her favorite pair looked like blue ovals. They were pretty and looked nice on her, too.

     A. buying a painting
     B. choosing eyeglasses
     C. Carol goes shopping

☐ **I can use details to determine the theme of a text.**
☐ **I can summarize the text.**
☐ **I can read and comprehend grade-level fiction text.**

Name_____

Read the story. Then, circle the phrase that completes each sentence.

Before the Atkins family began to pack for their vacation, they made a list of what they would need. Then, they laid out the needed clothes on the dining room table. They each had three pairs of shorts, three T-shirts, a swimming suit, socks, and shoes. They put their tents, sleeping bags, raincoats, flashlights, bug spray, cooking equipment, and fishing gear on the dining room floor.

1. The Atkins family's vacation was going ___ .

   to be in a warm climate

   to be in a city

2. On their vacation, they were _____ .

   going to eat out in restaurants

   going camping

3. The place they were going _____ .

   often had afternoon showers

   never had any bugs

4. They would be away _____ .

   for two weeks

   for a long weekend

They put the camping equipment and a duffel bag filled with their clothes in the car. They were off! In a couple of hours, they got to the campsite. After setting up camp, they headed for a swim. They ran shoeless to the water and jumped in. After swimming, they had to shower because they were muddy. They hung their suits on trees to dry. While Mom prepared dinner at the campsite, Dad and the children went back to the lake with their poles and bait.

5. The campsite was _____ .

   at the seashore

   in the woods

6. They swam _____ .

   in a swimming pool

   in a lake

7. The campsite was _____ .

   not too far from home

   first class

8. Dad and the children _____ .

   brought back fish

   fell in the pond

☐ I can use details and examples in a text to explain and draw inferences.
☐ I can use specific details from a text to describe a character, a setting, or an event.
☐ I can read and comprehend grade-level fiction text.

Use each dialogue to make an inference. Write the next part of the script.

1. Mom: Hi, Brian. How was school today?

   Brian: It was great. Wait until you hear about it. You are going to smile from ear to ear.

   Mom: I cannot wait to hear about your day. What happened?

   Brian: _____

   _____

   _____

2. Dad: Sean, are you awake?

   Sean: Wow, I am so tired! I almost fell asleep right here at the baseball game.

   Dad: Well, I am not surprised after last night.

   Sean: _____

   _____

   _____

3. Sandra: What time did Tina say that she would be here?

   Missy: She said that she would be here right after her soccer game. It should be any minute.

   Sandra: I wonder what her big surprise is. She said that it definitely involves us.

   Missy: She has been very sneaky lately, and I did hear her say something about a famous rock group.

   Tina: _____

   _____

☐ I can use details and examples in a text to explain and draw inferences.
☐ I can use dialogue and descriptions to enhance events and characters in a story.
☐ I can use descriptive words and details to help readers better understand a story.
☐ I can write a conclusion that completes a story.

Write the letter for the lesson that best describes the theme of each story.

A. If you are patient, your turn will come.

B. If you want to do well, keep practicing.

C. Being brave will help you achieve your goals.

_____ 1. Bethany's friends talked on the phone and traded glittery stickers. Each afternoon, they took turns deciding how to spend their time. Bethany did not always like the activity, but she played anyway. She knew that her turn would arrive soon.

_____ 2. Alex wanted to learn his multiplication tables. His friends knew how to multiply, and he wished that he could do it too. Each day, he spent one hour studying his flash cards. By the end of the month, Alex was a multiplication expert!

_____ 3. During the school play, Trey was scared to go on stage. But he took a deep breath and stepped onto the stage. He was a star!

Write a short story for each theme.

4. Telling the truth is very important. _____

_____

_____

_____

5. Everyone makes mistakes. _____

_____

_____

6. Even if you lose, you might learn a valuable lesson. _____

_____

_____

_____

☐ I can use details to determine the theme of a text.
☐ I can summarize the text.

Draw a picture for each setting.

1. Time: the future
   Place: a highway where everyone "drives" an airplane

2. Time: the day you were born
   Place: the hospital where you were born

3. Time: 6:00 pm
   Place: a busy restaurant

4. Time: today
   Place: a roller rink

5. Time: last Friday
   Place: a circus

6. Time: yesterday morning
   Place: a football game

☐ **I can use specific details from a text to describe a character, a setting, or an event.**

Read the story and follow the directions.

There was an old lady who lived on the edge of town. Everyone referred to her as Granny. Because she kept to herself, she seemed a little different to some. She asked nothing of anyone and did nothing for anyone except her many dogs. The number of dogs varied daily. Some dogs came only when they were hungry and left until they returned to eat again. Some knew that it was a good home and stayed.

One day, the paper boy noticed that Granny's papers had not been picked up for three or four days. The dogs in her yard were thin and looked almost lifeless as they moved about slowly. He had not seen Granny for about a week. He wondered if she was all right.

He got off his bike and walked up the steps onto the front porch. He walked around and peered in the windows, but he did not see anything. he opened the front door slightly and called, "Hello! Anyone here?" He listened for a minute. He thought that he heard a whimpering sound, so he quickly rode to the closest neighbor's house and called 911.

When the police arrived, they found that Granny had fallen and had not been able to move to call for help. The paramedics determined that Granny needed to go to the hospital, where she stayed for a few days.

While she was in the hospital, the paper boy came to feed her dogs every day. When Granny came home, neighbors brought food and flowers. Granny was sorry that she had not gotten to know her new friends sooner, but she was glad that she had now "found" them.

1. Circle what Granny's behavior indicates about her character at the beginning of the story.

She prefers to be alone.　　　She does not like people.　　　She is mean.

2. How does Granny's behavior change?

_____

3. Write three adjectives that describe the paper boy's character.

_____　_____　_____

☐ **I can use specific details from a text to describe a character, a setting, or an event.**
☐ **I can read and comprehend grade-level fiction text.**

Read the following passages and choose the point of view of each (first person, third person). Then, list the characters in the story, using the word *author* for stories written in the first person.

My family flies out tomorrow morning for a week's vacation at Yellowstone National Park. How exciting! But I have a problem. I am somewhat afraid of the wild animals that are allowed to roam free in the park. I know this is good for them, but the idea of meeting a buffalo or a bear or a gray wolf on one of the trails scares me to death. Please don't mention this to anyone.

1. Point of view _____

2. Characters in the story _____

Tony and Jose decided to order a different kind of pizza. Usually, they preferred sausage or pepperoni toppings. No veggies! No strange ingredients! They agreed to order every third ingredient from the list of possible choices until they had five items. When the list was complete, Tony looked at Jose and said, "You get the side with the anchovies and duck!" Jose wrinkled his nose and said, "Well, then you get the side with the red beets and green peas!"

3. Point of view _____

4. Characters in the story _____

When Erin made a list of kids to invite to her party, she thought about a couple of things. First, how many kids did she want for her party? If it is to be a sleep-over, she might only want four or five. If it is to be an outing at a frozen yogurt store, she might be allowed to invite a lot more. Then, she thought about who her best friends are. Whose feelings would be hurt if they aren't invited? Who might not want to come? And, who always invites her to their parties? There were lots of decisions to make.

5. Point of view _____

6. Characters in the story _____

☐ **I can compare and contrast the points of view from which different stories are narrated.**
☐ **I can read and comprehend grade-level fiction text.**

Use context clues to complete each sentence with one of the words in parentheses.

1. _____ is one of Tom's favorite subjects. (Astronaut, Astronomy, Atmosphere)

2. He _____ liked to follow the movement of the stars. (especially, establish, exceptionally)

3. When Tom was a little boy, his favorite outing was to visit a nearby _____. (platform, planetarium, planet)

4. Tom was delighted when his family gave him a _____. (telegram, telephoned, telescope)

5. Part of his birthday present was to go camping with his father in a park where _____ were good for stargazing. (constellations, conditions, conjunctions)

6. When the night came for Tom to go to the park, he took the necessary equipment with which to make his _____. (observes, orbits, observations)

7. Tom saw several _____, including Orion and the Dippers. (consultants, constellations, conformations)

8. Tom also saw the North Star, which is almost exactly _____ the north pole. (over, other, off)

9. He drew pictures of what he saw and recorded their positions using a _____. (compass, confess, congress)

10. He had a wonderful time and asked if his father would take him on another _____ to observe the stars. (explore, expedition, experience)

☐ I can figure out the meaning of words and phrases in a text using context clues.
☐ I can use context clues to understand an unfamiliar word or phrase.

Read the passage.

The Lighter Side of Time

The only reason for time is so that everything doesn't happen at once. (Albert Einstein)

"I'm going to fail science, Dad," Conner said.

"Why do you say that?"

"We're having a test on Einstein and his theory on time and space. I just don't understand him!"

Dad's face lit up with a huge smile. "Conner, when I was in college everyone in the math department used to say that even Einstein had a hard time understanding Einstein's Theory of Relativity. I learned a way to see what he was talking about, and even if you don't quite get it, it should help. Do you want to hear?"

"Sure, Dad. I'll try anything to pass this test."

"Imagine twin boys your age. Are you 16, yet?"

"You know I'm only 10."

"That's right! You're so smart I forgot how young you are. Well, anyway, one of the twins, Bob, stays home. The other twin, Bill, hops aboard a spaceship that can travel at the speed of light. That's 186,000 miles per second," Dad explained.

"Bill flies to Megagope, a planet 10 light-years from Earth. Once he gets there, he and the crew turn right around and head back home."

"No exploring or anything?" Conner said.

"Nope, no exploring. Meanwhile, 10 years have passed on Earth while Bill went to Megagope. Then, 10 more years passed while Bill returned to Earth. How old is Bob now?"

"That's easy! Bob was 10 years old plus the 10 years it took for the spaceship to get to the Megagope. That equals 20. Next, add the 10 years it took for Bill to come back to Earth. That makes Bob 30 years old. How old is Bill?"

"Good question, Conner. This is where you start to understand Einstein's Theory of Relativity. Since Bill traveled at speeds much faster than speeds you can travel on Earth, his body didn't age nearly as much as Bob's. Bill is still 10."

"So, let me see if I get this straight. Bill stays 10 because he was flying through space so fast, but Bob gets older by 20 years because he didn't go fast like Bill."

"That's right. Time passes differently depending on how fast you go. In Bill's case, the faster he went, the slower time passed."

"That means I could send an apple into space for 10 years, then send the apple back to Earth for another 10 years and still be able to have the apple for lunch 20 years from now."

"I think you'll pass your test," Dad said.

"Awesome!" Conner said.

☐ **I can read and comprehend grade-level fiction text.**

Follow the directions.

1. Number the events in the order they happened in "The Lighter Side of Time."

_____ Bill, age 10, comes back from Earth.

_____ Bob, age 10, stays on Earth.

_____ Bill's spaceship travels for 10 light-years to Megagope.

_____ Bob, Bill's twin, is now 30 years old.

2. Conner is 10 and sends an apple into space at the speed of light. The apple travels 15 light-years into space. It turns around and spends another 15 light-years coming back. The apple is only a couple of months old and still edible. How old will Conner be when he has it for lunch? _____

3. Write a comparison between Bob and Bill. Use the word *while* in your sentence.

_____

_____

Homophones are words that sound the same but have different meanings. Circle the correct homophone for each sentence.

4. The grandfather clock read 10 _____ 10.

passed   past

5. Cold filled the deep, dark _____ of space.

see   sea

6. Einstein, who loved to garden, thought it was fun to plant _____.

thyme   time

In each row, circle the word that does not belong.

7. joke	laugh	cry	smile
8. carrot	orange	peach	tangerine
9. huge	awesome	mammoth	large

10. Circle the best definition of *theory*.

fact   idea   proof

Write the base word for each word.

11. relativity _____   12. differently _____

13. studying _____   14. faster _____

☐ **I can use details and examples in a text to explain and draw inferences.**
☐ **I can figure out the meaning of words and phrases in a text using context clues.**
☐ **I can use prefixes, suffixes, and roots to understand unfamiliar words.**

Read the poems aloud to another person.

'Tis Midnight

1   'Tis midnight, and the setting sun
        Is slowly rising in the west;
    The rapid rivers slowly run,
        The frog is on his downy nest.
    The pensive goat and sportive cow
        Hilarious, leap from bough to bough.

Anonymous

The Train Pulled in the Station

2   O, the train pulled in the station,
        The bell was ringing wet;
    The track ran by the depot,
        And I think it's running yet.

3   'Twas midnight on the ocean,
        Not a streetcar was in sight;
    The sun and moon were shining,
        And it rained all day that night.

4   'Twas a summer day in winter,
        And the snow was raining fast;
    As a barefoot boy, with shoes on,
        Stood, sitting on the grass.

5   O, I jumped into the river,
        Just because it had a bed;
    I took a sheet of water
        For to cover up my head.

6   O, the rain makes all things beautiful,
        The flowers and grasses too;
    If the rain makes all things beautiful,
        Why don't it rain on you?

An American Folk Song

I can read and comprehend grade-level fiction text.

Refer back to the poem on page 22, "The Train Pulled in the Station." For each stanza, write one thing that doesn't make sense.

1. Stanza 1 _____

2. Stanza 2 _____

3. Stanza 3 _____

4. Stanza 4 _____

5. Stanza 5 _____

Write what you think is the silliest part of "'Tis Midnight." Be sure to tell why you think it's silly.

6. _____

_____

Write the words that make up the compound words found in the stanzas in parentheses.

7. (3) _____ and _____,

_____ and _____

8. (4) _____ and _____

Check the meaning of the underlined homograph as it is used in the sentence.

9. <u>Dates</u> are often used when making muffins.

_____ a kind of fruit   _____ a day in a month

10. The holy man went on a <u>fast</u>.

_____ swift moving   _____ a period of not eating food

11. Cheese can <u>age</u> rapidly.

_____ to grow old   _____ long period of time

12. It was almost more than his mother could <u>bear</u>.

_____ put up with   _____ a large omnivorous animal

☐ **I can use proper terms to explain the differences between poems, drama, and prose.**
☐ **I can correctly use frequently confused words such as to, too, and two.**

Read the story below. Illustrate your favorite part of the story and write a caption for it.

The Crow Who Brought the Daylight (An Inuit Story)

Long ago when the earth was first born, the Inuit people from the north lived in darkness. They did not mind because they thought everyone lived in darkness. But one day an old crow let something slip. He had flown all around the world and had seen daylight many times on his travels. When the Inuit people heard about daylight, they wanted it too.

"Think about all of the things we could do if we had daylight," the people said. "We could travel far. We would be safer. We could see polar bears coming. We could catch more fish." The people asked the old crow to fly out and bring them back daylight. He said that he was too old and too tired. But the people continued to beg. Finally Crow agreed.

Crow flew east for a long time. He had nearly given up when he saw a faint flicker of daylight ahead of him. "Ah," said the tired crow. "There's the daylight the people want." As he continued flying, the sky got brighter and brighter. He finally landed in a tree near a river. He needed to rest after his long journey.

Crow watched a village girl take water from the river. Hoping to get warm, he turned himself into a speck of dust and floated down onto her warm fur coat. When she returned to her father's snow home, Crow floated off the girl's coat and into her young brother's ear. The boy started to cry.

"What's wrong?" his father asked.

"Ask for a ball of daylight to play with," the speck of dust whispered.

The father was glad to give his favorite son a ball of daylight. He wanted him to be happy, and he had plenty of balls of daylight. The boy took the ball of daylight and left his snow home to play outside. That quickly, the speck of dust turned back into Crow again. He grabbed the ball of daylight in his claws and flew quickly up into the bright sky, heading west back to his people.

When he reached the land of the Inuit again, the people were waiting for him. "Quick!" they exclaimed. "Give us daylight!"

"I could only bring one ball back," Crow said. "There is only enough for half the year." The people didn't mind. They were glad for any daylight at all.

Crow dropped the ball to the ground, where it splintered into a thousand pieces of daylight. As the pieces shone upward, the land of the Inuit became bright and beautiful. The people could see for miles and miles. What a beautiful homeland they had!

☐ **I can read and comprehend grade-level fiction text.**

Answer the questions with complete sentences.

1. On the previous page, draw an illustration for the story. Write a caption beneath it.

2. What are three things you could not do if you lived in total darkness?

_____

_____

3. Why do you think Crow was willing to go on such a long journey?

_____

_____

4. What would be the advantage to being able to change your shape like Crow did when he changed himself into a speck of dust. Explain.

_____

_____

_____

5. Do you think a ball of daylight would be heavy or light? Explain.

_____

_____

6. Where do the Inuit people live? Use reference materials if you need to.

_____

_____

_____

☐ **I can use details and examples in a text to explain and draw inferences.**
☐ **I can use specific details from a text to describe a character, a setting, or an event.**
☐ **I can use illustrations to support what I know about a text.**

Read the summary of *Shiloh* by Phyllis Reynolds Naylor (Aladdin, 2000). Use details from the summary to complete the puzzle. The bold spaces will tell you what award this book received.

    In *Shiloh*, an award-winning book, 11-year-old Marty Preston tells about what happens when a dog follows him home. Marty lives with his parents and two sisters, Becky and Dara Lynn, in the hills above Friendly. Friendly is a small town in West Virginia near Sisterville. On a Sunday afternoon, after a big dinner of rabbit and sweet potatoes, Marty goes for a walk along the river. During his walk, Marty spies a short-haired dog. The dog, a beagle with black and brown spots, does not make a sound as he watches and follows Marty. From the dog's behavior, Marty suspects that the dog has been mistreated. Since he found the dog near the old Shiloh schoolhouse, Marty calls the dog Shiloh. Marty soon discovers that Shiloh belongs to mean Judd Travers. After returning Shiloh to Judd, Marty contemplates how he can earn enough money to buy the dog. Before Marty can solve this problem, he is faced with a difficult decision.

1. In what town does Marty live?

2. How old is Marty?

3. What kind of potatoes does the family eat on Sunday?

4. What kind of meat do they eat?

5. What kind of dog is Shiloh?

6. Write the last name of Shiloh's owner.

7. Name one of Marty's sisters.

8. What adjective is used to describe Judd Travers?

9. What is Marty's last name?

10. On what day does Marty find Shiloh?

11. Who tells the story?

12. Marty finds the dog by what schoolhouse?

☐ **I can read and comprehend grade-level fiction text.**

© Carson-Dellosa • CD-104611

Name_____

This book summary is about the much beloved book *Old Yeller* by Fred Gipson (Scholastic Book Services, 1957). *Old Yeller* won a number of awards, including the 1957 Newbery Honor Book award.

Old Yeller is about a boy and a dog. When Travis's father left to take their cattle to market, young Travis had to take his father's place on the farm. This required him to plow the fields, chop wood, hunt for food for the dinner table, take care of the livestock, and protect his mother and little brother. This was a lot of responsibility for young Travis and sometimes he did not feel up to it. In the middle of all this, an ugly yellow dog showed up on the farm. At first, Travis hated the dog for stealing the family's meager supply of meat. But later, after the dog saved his little brother from an angry mother bear, Travis came to appreciate the dog's protection and help. He named the dog Old Yeller and the dog became his closest friend. At the end of the story, Old Yeller was bitten by a rabid wolf and Travis had a hard decision to make.

Compare and contrast what you read about *Old Yeller* with the summary of *Shiloh* on the previous page.

1. What are some qualities that Shiloh and Old Yeller have in common?

   _____

   _____

2. Compare and contrast how the two boys met the dogs that were to become their best friends.

   _____

   _____

3. Tell what you know or might guess about the difficult decisions both Marty and Travis had to make at the end of these books.

   _____

   _____

   _____

☐ I can use specific details from a text to describe a character, a setting, or an event.
☐ I can compare and contrast the points of view from which different stories are narrated.
☐ I can compare and contrast themes, topics, and patterns of events in various texts.

Read the supporting sentences and circle the main idea they support.

1. A. Farming was not always as efficient as it is today.

    B. Sometimes, disease or bad weather ruined the crops before they were ready to harvest. Therefore, when there was a good harvest, people had a reason to celebrate.

    People would be hungry if there was a poor crop.

    Today, farmers use fertilizer to grow better crops.

    Long ago, festivals were held when there was a good harvest.

2. A. They gave thanks because they had a good harvest.

    B. The crops they gathered are now part of an American Thanksgiving feast. Traditional Thanksgiving foods include turkey, cranberry sauce, and pumpkin pie.

    The Native Americans helped the settlers plant seeds.

    The first European settlers in America had a fall festival that they named Thanksgiving.

    Turkey and harvested crops are served on Thanksgiving.

3. A. Although farming has changed, the harvest is still celebrated.

    B. Different communities and countries celebrate in different ways. Some religious groups offer fruits and vegetables to the needy.

    Food is now grown in greenhouses all year round.

    Nearly all farmers today harvest their crops with machines.

    There is usually a celebration of some sort after a harvest.

☐ **I can use details and examples in a text to explain and draw inferences.**
☐ **I can use details to determine the theme of and summarize the text.**

Read the following passage and complete the activity below.

Ancient civilizations did not have scientific information that explained the causes of earthquakes. They made up stories that reveal their lack of understanding. One belief of some of these ancient people was that Earth was carried on the backs of animals.

Some Native Americans thought that a giant sea turtle held up Earth. They believed that when the turtle moved, Earth moved. When the turtle moved more, Earth moved more, causing cracks to form on Earth's surface.

In India, it was believed that four elephants held up Earth. They stood on the back of a turtle, and the turtle, in turn, balanced on the back of a snake. If any of these animals moved, Earth would shake and cause an earthquake. The greater the movement was, the greater the earthquake was.

The ancient Greeks thought that earthquakes showed the gods' anger. A giant, named Atlas, had rebelled against the gods, so he had to hold the world on his shoulders as punishment. The Greeks believed that any time Atlas adjusted Earth's weight on his shoulders, an earthquake followed.

Write the main idea of the passage. Then, write a supporting idea from each of the last three paragraphs.

1. _____

_____

2. _____

_____

3. _____

_____

4. _____

_____

☐ I can use details and examples from a text to explain and draw inferences.
☐ I can tell the main idea of a text and use key ideas to support it.
☐ I can summarize the text.
☐ I can explain how the author uses evidence to support the ideas in a text.

Read the passage. Then, answer the questions below.

Lobsters are saltwater animals belonging to a group called crustaceans. A lobster has a hard outer shell and five sets of legs. The first set of legs are known as claws. One is usually used for crushing and the other for biting. The female lobster lays thousands of eggs, and the tiny young drift and swim for three to five weeks before settling on the bottom of the ocean.

Crayfish are freshwater versions of their crustacean cousins called lobsters. Crawfish, as they are also called, may be as short as two inches (five centimeters) in length. Like their cousins, crayfish have large front claws that are actually one of five sets of legs. Crayfish are found around the world, except in Africa and Antarctica, in freshwater rivers and streams.

1. What would be a good title for this passage?

    A. River Animals
    B. Lobsters
    C. Cousins with Claws

2. What is the topic sentence of the first paragraph?

    A. The first set of legs are known as claws.
    B. A lobster has a hard outer shell and five sets of legs.
    C. Lobsters are saltwater animals belonging to a group called crustaceans.

3. What is the topic sentence of the second paragraph?

    A. Crawfish, as they are also called, may be as short as two inches (five centimeters) in length.
    B. Crayfish are freshwater versions of their crustacean cousins called lobsters.
    C. Crayfish are found in freshwater rivers and streams.

☐ I can tell the main idea of a text and use key details to support it.
☐ I can read and comprehend grade-level informational text.

Read the passage and complete the puzzle.

Mark Spitz is an American swimmer who set an Olympic record when he won seven gold medals at the 1972 Summer Olympics in Germany. Mark had been swimming races since he was eight years old. By his late teens, he had already broken three world records in the freestyle and butterfly races. At the 1968 Summer Olympics in Mexico, Mark hoped to win the gold medal, but he did not swim his best. He finished second in the butterfly and third in the freestyle. With heavy training, Mark Spitz came to the 1972 Olympics ready to swim his best. And, did he ever!

Across

3. What country did Mark represent?

4. How old was Mark when he began swimming races?

6. Where were the Olympics held when Mark did not swim his best?

7. How many gold medals did Mark win in 1972?

Down

1. Which swimming stroke was Mark's best at the Olympics in Mexico?

2. Where were the Olympics held when Mark won seven gold medals?

5. How many world records did Mark set as a teenager?

☐ I can use details and examples from a text to explain and draw inferences.
☐ I can read and comprehend grade-level informational text.

Read the information. Then, complete the chart.

Mollusks belong to a large family of invertebrate animals. Animals that belong to this group usually have soft, one-sectioned bodies that are covered by hard shells. A person walking on a beach might find several of their discarded shells. Animals once lived in these seashells.

Biologists divide mollusks into seven groups called classes, but only some of the mollusks have hard protective shells. Gastropoda is one class of mollusks. Most often, a gastropod has a single, coiled shell. Included in this class are limpets, slugs, snails, and whelks. They can be found on the beaches of the Atlantic and Pacific Oceans in North America.

Bivalves is another large class of mollusks. The shell of a bivalve is actually two shells hinged together at one end or along one side. The animals that call these shells home include clams, oysters, mussels, and scallops. They too can be found on both coasts of North America.

A third class of mollusks are chitons. A chiton's body is covered by eight shell plates that look something like a turtle's shell. Merten's chiton, northern red chiton, and mossy mopalia are all included in this class. Chitons generally live in shallow rock pools. They can be found along the shores of the Pacific Ocean from Alaska to Mexico.

	Gastropods	Bivalves	Chitons
What do their shells look like?			
Where can they be found?			
List mollusks included in each class.			

☐ I can use details and examples from a text to explain and draw inferences.
☐ I can read and comprehend grade-level informational text.

Dinosaurs lived long ago—about 60 million years ago. Today, all that is left of them are their fossils, bones, and footprints. But, what does 60 million years mean to us? A geologic time scale was developed by scientists that illustrates the periods in Earth's history. It can help those of us living today gain some perspective about the time involved in the development of life on Earth.

Read the chart and answer the questions.

1. Earth's history is divided into how many major eras? _____

2. What are the era's names?

_____

3. In which era did the dinosaurs exist?

_____

_____

4. Into how many periods is the Mesozoic era divided?

_____

5. What are the Mesozoic periods' names?

_____

6. In which era do you live?

_____

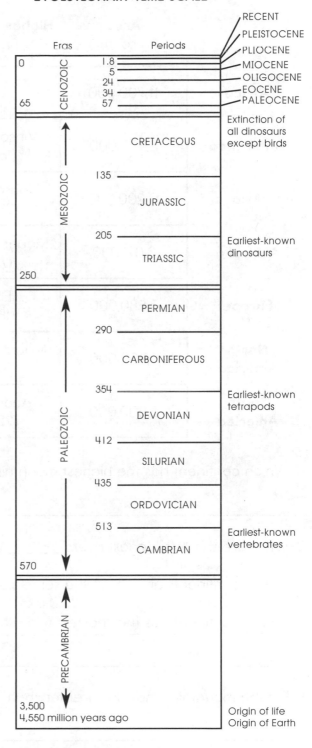

GEOLOGIC AND EVOLUTIONARY TIME SCALE

- ☐ I can explain the way a text is organized.
- ☐ I can use the visuals in a text to better understand the subject.
- ☐ I can explain how the visuals support the text.
- ☐ I can read and comprehend grade-level informational text.

Name_____

Use the chart to answer the questions.

	Area (in sq. mi.)	Highest Mountain (in feet)	Lowest Point (feet below sea level)	Longest River (in miles)
Africa	11,700,000	Kilimanjaro (19,340)	Lake Assal (512)	Nile (4,145)
Antarctica	5,400,000	Vinson Massif (16,864)	not known	no rivers
Asia	17,200,000	Mount Everest (29,028)	Dead Sea (1,312)	Yangtze (3,915)
Australia	3,071,000	Mount Kosciusko (7,310)	Lake Eyre (52)	Murray-Darling (2,310)
Europe	3,580,000	Elbrus (18,510)	Caspian Sea (92)	Volga (2,194)
North America	9,400,000	Mount McKinley (20,320)	Death Valley (282)	Missouri (2,540)
South America	6,900,000	Aconcagua (22,834)	Valdes Peninsula (131)	Amazon (4,000)

1. Which continent has the highest mountain and the lowest point?

_____

2. What are the two longest rivers? _____

3. Which continents are about the same size? _____

4. Which continent has the shortest mountain and the highest lowest point?

_____

5. List the mountains that are greater than 20,000 feet high.

_____

☐ I can use the visuals in a text to better understand the subject.
☐ I can explain how the visuals support the text.
☐ I can read and comprehend grade-level informational text.

Read the passage. Then, write each bold word next to its definition below.

Food for Survival

The rocky land of the northern forests in North America was never good for farming. Without fish and game, the early **natives** would have starved. Their lives were **contingent** on the animals they hunted.

In order to survive, the early Native Americans of the North American forests played games that **incorporated** the skills they needed to be successful in their **culture**. They needed to be able to judge distances, pick up clues and signs from their environment, and conceal themselves from the animals they hunted. In one of the games the Native Americans played, the men threw axes. In another, they took turns throwing spears or sticks into a hoop on the ground. Such games improved the players' **accuracy**.

Moose and caribou were very important to the tribes. Moose usually lived and traveled by themselves. Caribou migrated in herds covering a large territory each season. The Native Americans **stalked** the moose from one **range** to another, but when hunting caribou, they would wait for them at a place along the caribou's trails.

Weirs, nets, traps, hooks, and spears were used to catch fish. Whitefish and jackfish were caught in lakes, and Arctic grayling and trout were caught in rivers. The Native Americans fished from the shore or in canoes in summer and through holes cut in the ice in winter.

After the ice melted, the traps were set. Sometimes, the Native Americans would discover a bear still hibernating in its den. Such a kill would feed the camp for a few days. Sometimes, when meat was scarce, the Native Americans would eat rabbit, mink, or wolverine. When hunting became poor, they lived on dried meat and fish and on pemmican, a mixture of dried meat and animal fat.

1. open area on which animals roam _____

2. combined into one body _____

3. original inhabitants _____

4. dependent upon _____

5. pursued prey _____

6. quality of being exact _____

7. enclosures set in a waterway for catching fish _____

8. one's social group _____

☐ **I can figure out the meaning of words or phrases in informational text.**
☐ **I can read and comprehend grade-level informational text.**
☐ **I can use context clues to understand an unfamiliar word or phrase.**

Read the story. Then follow the directions on the following page.

Gerbils can be wonderful pets. But, like any pet, they require commitment. New owners must consider if they have the time and the motivation to give good care. It is important to consider timing, money, and circumstances.

Gerbils weigh from 60 to 100 grams, about the same as half a medium baked potato. They grow to be about four inches long. Their tails are around the same length. They come in different colors, but most of them have white fur on their stomachs. They can live up to four years.

The basics for setting up a gerbil as a pet at home include a cage, gerbil food, toys and treats, and litter and bedding materials. It will cost money to raise a healthy and happy gerbil. A cage can cost $25 or more. A year's worth of gerbil food, toys, litter and bedding can cost $300 or more. Veterinarian bills can add up. Save your allowance!

Gerbils are busy little creatures. They can be very active and love to play. Gerbil toys such as exercise wheels, play tubes, ladders, and run-around balls offer these playful pets hours of fun. Gerbils love to dig. They can get hours of tunneling fun in extra bedding, shredded paper towels, or hay.

It is helpful to remember that gerbils are social creatures. Buying them two at a time can add to the happy gerbil home. They should be introduced to each other while young to make certain they get along. Ideally, the two will come from the same family. Remember not to pair a female and male to avoid litters of new gerbils.

Gerbil food is usually made up of grain, seeds, pellets, and dried vegetables. Gerbils especially find sunflower seeds tasty treats, so they may pick these out and eat them first! It is also recommended that gerbils receive small bits of chopped vegetables such as lettuce, carrots, and broccoli. Because a rodent's teeth grow continuously, it needs something to gnaw on to wear them down. A sterile bone or safe twig should be included in its daily fare. And, like all pets, gerbils need a good supply of fresh water, changed daily.

A pet gerbil can offer hours of fun and lots of cuddles. They are small creatures and must be handled carefully, but with daily care and attention, they are soon a valued part of the family.

☐ **I can read and comprehend grade-level informational text.**

After reading the passage on page 36, interview someone who owns or has owned a gerbil. Ask these questions:

1. When did you get a gerbil? _____

2. Did you like having a gerbil for a pet? _____

3. Was it a lot of work or was it easy to take care of a gerbil? _____

4. What did your gerbil eat? _____

5. Did your gerbil like to play? With what? _____

6. Did it cost much to take care of a pet gerbil? _____

7. What didn't you like about owning a gerbil? _____

8. Would you recommend a gerbil for a pet? _____

Now, write a paragraph to compare and contrast the passage on page 36 with the facts you learned in your interview. Which gave you the best information?

_____

_____

_____

_____

_____

_____

_____

_____

☐ I can compare and contrast two different accounts of the same event or topic.
☐ I can consider the purpose and the audience when writing.
☐ I can research different aspects of a topic.

Write the letter for each effect.

1. After the tsunami hit Japan, _____

2. When kids are bullied, _____

3. If you don't floss your teeth, _____

4. Fewer people buy from stores _____

5. While traveling in large cities with the windows down, _____

6. When you sit in the back seat of the bus, _____

7. The airport was closed _____

8. A solar eclipse happens when _____

9. Hundreds of people were stranded _____

10. Many people go to the emergency room _____

11. After Harriet Tubman fled slavery, _____

12. Yeast produces gas in bread, _____

13. Helen Keller had a childhood illness _____

14. Peer pressure _____

15. Good test grades are easier to get _____

A. due to heavy rain and poor visibility.

B. when doctor's offices are closed.

C. they become depressed and unhappy.

D. if you study before tests.

E. can make students uncomfortable.

F. the ride will be bumpier.

G. because of heavy snow fall.

H. that left her deaf and blind.

I. she helped rescue other slaves.

J. many people donated food and clothing.

K. causing it to rise.

L. since it became easy to shop online.

M. you might get cavities.

N. the moon moves between the earth and the sun.

O. you can often smell air pollution.

☐ I can identify cause and effect.

Read the passage. Then, write a paragraph comparing and contrasting the two players.

Michael Jordan grew up in North Carolina. His father built a basketball court in the backyard for all of his children to use. Michael enjoyed all sports, but basketball was his favorite. Michael tried to make his high school's varsity team as a sophomore, but the coach thought that he was too short. However, by his junior year, he had grown and sharpened his basketball skills, and he make the varsity team. The rest is history: he got a scholarship to the University of North Carolina, won the national championship for the university, helped the United States Olympic basketball team win a gold medal, and became a Chicago Bull. Michael Jordan broke many National Basketball Association (NBA) records and received several Most Valuable Player (MVP) awards. He retired from basketball and tried playing baseball, but after two years, he returned to playing basketball and set even more records.

Kareem Abdul-Jabbar was born Ferdinand Lewis "Lew" Alcindor Jr. He was born and raised in the New York City area. Early on, he had a passion for music and baseball. Not until the summer between first and second grade did he first pick up a basketball. In eighth grade, he helped his junior high win the district championship. Lew made the high school varsity team his freshman year, and the rest is history: he led his high school to record-setting winning streaks, received a scholarship to the University of California at Los Angeles, and led the team to three titles while receiving three MVP awards. During his college years, he changed his name to Kareem Abdul-Jabbar. He also boycotted the 1968 Olympics. He and other US athletes decided a boycott would send a message about racism in the United States. After college, he was drafted by the Milwaukee Bucks and was traded six years later to the Los Angeles Lakers. For both teams, he had personal and team successes. He was voted MVP five times. He was the NBA's leading scorer and led both teams to national championships.

_____

_____

_____

_____

_____

_____

_____

☐ I can use information from two sources to write or talk about a subject.
☐ I can read and comprehend grade-level informational text.

Read the passage.

Taking Care of Teeth

Long ago, people cleaned their teeth in many interesting ways. They scratched their teeth with sticks, wiped them with rags, or even chewed on crushed bones or shells. Tooth care has come a long way in the past few hundred years. Now we have fluoride toothpaste, dental floss, and specially angled toothbrushes to keep our teeth healthy.

It took someone with a lot of time on his hands to invent the first toothbrush. In the 1770s, a man named William Addis was in prison. While he was wiping his teeth with a rag, he had the idea to make a tool for cleaning teeth. He used a bone and some bristles from a hairbrush. He carefully drilled holes in one end of the bone. Then, he trimmed the brush bristles and pushed them into the holes that he had drilled. He glued the bristles into place and had made the first toothbrush.

People have used different tooth cleaners over the years. Many cleaners, such as crushed bones and shells, actually damaged the protective enamel on teeth. Chalk was a popular cleaner in the 1850s. Baking soda was also used for many years because it was abrasive. Some toothpastes still contain baking soda. Other people used salt as a tooth cleaner. Many of today's toothpastes contain sodium too. Fluoride was first added to toothpaste in 1956. Fluoride greatly reduced the number of cavities in children. More recently, calcium was added to toothpaste in the 1960s to help strengthen teeth.

Using dental floss once a day is one of the most important things that you can do for your teeth. Originally, the thin string was made of silk. Now, dental floss comes in different colors and flavors, tape, and waxed and unwaxed varieties. Dental floss removes "interproximal plaque accumulation," which means that it scrapes off the plaque between your teeth where a toothbrush cannot reach.

The inventions and improvements in dental care have helped people maintain stronger, healthier teeth. We now know how to care for our teeth every day.

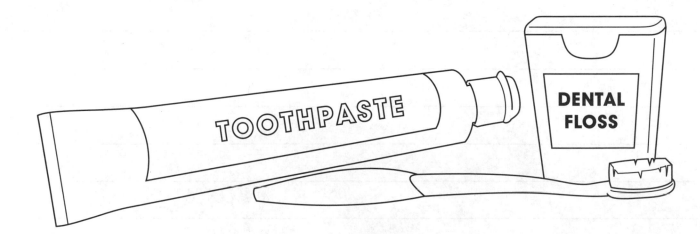

☐ I can read and comprehend grade-level informational text.

Use the passage on page 40 to answer the questions.

Taking Care of Teeth

1. Why did the author write this passage?

    A. to entertain

    B. to teach

    C. to sell something

2. What kind of passage is "Taking Care of Teeth"?

    A. a factual passage

    B. a humorous passage

    C. a fictional passage

3. Why was calcium added to toothpaste? _____

_____

4. What does fluoride do? _____

_____

5. Complete the diagram with details from the passage.

The Importance of Dental Floss

A. _____

_____

William Addis

A. _____

B. _____

Tooth Care

Tooth Cleaners Over the Years

A. _____

B. _____

C. _____

Tooth Cleaning Today

A. _____

B. _____

C. _____

☐ **I can use details and examples from a text to explain and draw inferences.**
☐ **I can use specific information in nonfiction text to explain the main idea.**
☐ **I can figure out the meaning of words and phrases in informational text.**

Read the passage. Then, read the poems.

Day Poetry

Robert Louis Stevenson was born on November 13, 1850, in Edinburgh, Scotland. He grew up in a wealthy family and received an excellent education from private tutors. His father was an engineer who designed magnificent lighthouses along the rocky coastline of Scotland. Stevenson knew that his father wanted him to become an engineer too. But, Robert had a different idea.

By the time Stevenson was 17 years old, he had decided to become a writer. Reading about traveling had recently become popular in Europe. Luckily for him, he liked to travel. By writing for travel magazines, Stevenson, was able to have the best of what he loved. He could write and get paid by a publisher to travel to wonderful places.

At first, Stevenson wrote for adults. Then, in 1881, he was on vacation along the shores of Scotland with his family. They had the misfortune of rainy weather the entire vacation. While cooped up in a house with teenagers, he began to write *Treasure Island*. When the book was published and sold out at stores all over Great Britain, Stevenson knew that he should write for children. He also wrote a book of poetry called *A Child's Garden of Verses*.

Stevenson spent years traveling through Europe and as far away as California. His travels made him aware of time and the objects in the sky. These are subjects of many of his stories and poems.

The Sun's Travels

The sun is not a-bed when I
At night upon my pillow lie;
Still round the earth his way he takes,
And morning after morning makes.
While here at home, in shining day,
We round the sunny garden play,
Each little Indian sleepy-head
Is being kissed and put to bed.
And when at eve I rise from tea,
Day dawns beyond the Atlantic Sea;
And all the children in the West
Are getting up and being dressed.

Time to Rise

A birdie with a yellow bill
Hopped upon the window sill,
Cocked his shining eye and said:
"Ain't you 'shamed, you sleepy-head?"

☐ I can read and comprehend grade-level fiction text.
☐ I can read and comprehend grade-level informational text.

Use the passage and the poems on page 42 to answer the questions.

Day Poetry

1. What does being "cooped up" mean? _____

_____

2. What does the coast of Scotland look like? _____

_____

3. Write an opinion from the story. _____

_____

4. What did Robert Louis Stevenson love to do? _____

_____

5. Name the title of Stevenson's book of poetry. _____

6. Why do you think that the bird asked, "Ain't you 'shamed, you sleepy-head?"

_____

_____

7. Why is the sun not "a-bed" in "The Sun's Travels"? _____

_____

Circle the word that does not belong in each row.

8. publisher	author	writer	tourist
9. England	Europe	Ireland	Scotland
10. newspaper	magazine	popcorn	journal
11. tutor	playmate	teacher	instructor

Write an antonym for each word.

12. days _____

13. wonderful _____

14. best _____

15. wealthy _____

☐ I can use details and examples from a text to explain and draw inferences.
☐ I can use context clues to understand an unfamiliar word or phrase.
☐ I can use antonyms and synonyms to better understand words.

Read the poem. Then, read the passage.

Days of the Week

Monday's Child

Monday's child is fair of face,
Tuesday's child is full of **grace**,
Wednesday's child will fear no foe,
Thursday's child has far to go,
Friday's child is loving and giving,
Saturday's child works hard for a living,
But a child that's born on the Sabbath day
Is **bonny** and **blithe** and good in every way.

Anonymous

No one seems to agree on the **origin** of the seven-day week. Many historians believe that the Babylonians were the first to break the year into months. At some point in history, in became important to divide the year into smaller parts. Around 1600 BC, a new period of time was created. It was longer than a day, but less than a month. This was called the week.

A lunar month is the time that it takes the moon to complete a cycle from new moon to new moon. A lunar month is 29 1/2 days. One reason a week is seven days long is because four seven-day weeks are close to the amount of time in a lunar month.

Different **cultures** have had different names for the days of the week. However, names of the month are similar in many languages.

In ancient times, people could see seven "planets" in the sky without a telescope. They saw the sun, the moon, Mars, Mercury, Jupiter, Venus, and Saturn. (No one had studied the sky with a telescope until Galileo in the sixteenth century. Until then, people thought that the sun and the moon were planets.)

Many languages connect each day of the week with one of these planets. In English, you can find these planet names in Monday, Saturday, and Sunday. The other four days have been substituted with the names of Nordic and Anglo-Saxon gods.

English	French	Planet
Monday	lundi	moon
Tuesday	mardi	Mars
Wednesday	mercredi	Mercury
Thursday	jeudi	Jupiter
Friday	vendredi	Venus
Saturday	samedi	Saturn
Sunday	dimanche	sun

☐ **I can read and comprehend grade-level fiction text.**
☐ **I can read and comprehend grade-level informational text.**

Use the poem and the passage on page 44 to answer the questions.

Days of the Week

1. Write the sentence from the passage that tells when people began to use instruments to look at the sky. _____

_____

_____

2. What is the French word for Thursday? _____

3. What are the names of the "planets" that could be seen without a telescope?

_____

4. What planet was Saturday named after? _____

5. Describe the child born on Friday. _____

_____

Write the letter of the definition on the line next to its matching word. Use a dictionary for help.

6. _____ bonny   A. merry

7. _____ grace   B. beginning

8. _____ blithe   C. attractive

9. _____ culture   D. a civilization

10. _____ origin   E. having charm

Complete the outline with details from the passage.

11. Months and weeks

   A. Babylonians separate years into months.

   B. _____

12. Names of days

   A. Ancient people named days after planets.

   B. _____

☐ I can use details and examples from a text to explain and draw inferences.
☐ I can figure out the meaning of words or phrases in informational text.
☐ I can use the visuals in a text to better understand the subject.

Read the passage.

Migration

When large groups of animals move from one place to another and back again, it is called migration. Birds, butterflies, elk, whales, salmon, and plankton are just some of the animals that migrate. Scientists are still studying what makes animals do this. They know two things for sure: daylight and temperature changes have important effects on animal movement.

Humans used to migrate from cool northern mountains to warmer southerly plains as the seasons changed. But, now we have well-insulated houses with furnaces to keep us warm and air conditioners to keep us cool. A foot of snow could cover our lawns, and we could still go to the store to buy fresh vegetables.

Until about 100 years ago, American Indians migrated with the seasons. As daylight grew longer and snow began to melt, the Shoshone would pack their homes and move north. Sometimes, they went as far north as Canada. Then, as the maple leaves turned **crimson**, the Shoshone would gather nuts and berries. The men would hunt migrating deer, elk, and rabbits for food and thick winter coats. The women would dry the meat and prepare the skins for clothing. When they were ready, some Shoshone tribes would **trek** south into warm desert lands.

In the western United States, ranchers herd cattle and sheep into the high **mesas** for summer **grazing**. Shepherds, with their colorful wagons, can occasionally be seen watching the flocks. In the fall, ranchers drive the animals to the valley floors for **overwintering**.

One interesting migratory animal is the plankton. Plankton are simple-celled creatures that are ruled by the sun. They are a major food source for other ocean animals. The enormous blue whale eats almost nothing but plankton. As daylight touches the surface of the ocean, plankton sink deeper into the water, away from sunlight. Later in the day, as night approaches, the plankton slowly rise to the surface.

On March 19, swallows arrive to rebuild their nests in the ruins of an old stone church. The church is in the little village of San Juan Capistrano along the coast of California. Each March, the town is overrun by visitors who come to see this "miracle of nature."

Scout swallows arrive a few days ahead of the main flock. They circle the roofless building and then fly off to lead the rest of the swallows home. On October 23, the swallows take flight and head for a warmer climate.

Legend says that when the swallows first land in the spring, the giant yellow flowers of the *celandine* (sel-un-deen) plant burst open. Then, as the last swallow flies away in the autumn, the plants **wither** and fall to the ground.

☐ **I can read and comprehend grade-level informational text.**

Migration

Use the passage on page 46 to answer the questions.

1. What is the name of the flower that bursts open when the swallows arrive?

    a. tomatoes

    b. berries

    c. celandine

2. Which animal did the Shoshone hunt?

    a. moose

    b. elk

    c. cougars

3. What is the topic of this passage?

    a. swallows

    b. migration

    c. plankton

4. What is a major cause for migration?

    a. the moon

    b. daylight

    c. ocean tides

Write the letter of the definition on the line next to its matching word. Use a dictionary for help.

5. _____ wither   A. to travel or migrate

6. _____ trek   B. a deep red

7. _____ mesa   C. to shrink or wilt

8. _____ crimson   D. to eat

9. _____ overwinter   E. a flat-topped hill

10. _____ grazing   F. to keep something alive from autumn to spring

☐ **I can use details and examples from a text to explain and draw inferences.**
☐ **I can tell the main idea of a text and use key details to support it.**
☐ **I can summarize the text.**
☐ **I can figure out the meanings of words or phrases in informational text.**

Draw lines to match the prefix with its meaning, then another line to an example. Use a dictionary for help if you need it.

1. anti-	A. before	a. bicycle
2. bi-	B. after	b. introduction
3. intro-	C. half	c. semicircle
4. micro-	D. against	d. multicultural
5. multi-	E. many	e. nonreader
6. non-	F. three	f. antibiotic
7. post-	G. not	g. microchip
8. pre-	H. again	h. previous
9. re-	I. small	i. unnecessary
10. semi-	J. two	j. recreate
11. tri-	K. inward	k. postwar
12. un-	L. not	l. tricycle

☐ **I can use my knowledge of letter sounds, syllables, and word parts to read unfamiliar words.**
☐ **I can read with accuracy, fluency, and expression.**

Write the words from the word bank in the column to show the correct number of syllables.

tissue	transparent	soaring	mate
migratory	jaws	finally	caterpillars
hatch	nectar	bothersome	honeysuckle

1 syllable	2 syllables	3 syllables	4 syllables

Use context clues in the sentences to help you fill in the blanks. Each word will be used only once.

1. A monarch butterfly is nearly _____ in the sunlight and as thin as _____ paper.

2. She feeds on _____ and water during her _____ trip south to avoid the frigid winters in the northern United States.

3. After _____ southward for two months, the monarch _____ arrives at her winter home.

4. As the days get longer and warmer, the monarch butterflies _____. Then, the females begin their flight north.

5. A female will lay as many as 500 eggs on milkweed plants across the United States. Then, _____ will _____ from the butterfly eggs.

6. Butterflies do not have _____ to chew with. They sip nectar from flowers using a straw-like mouth.

7. Although gardeners think milkweed is a _____ plant, these are the only leaves that the monarch caterpillar eats.

8. Many flowers attract monarch butterflies, such as marigolds, zinnias, sunflowers, and _____.

☐ **I can use my knowledge of letter sounds, syllables, and word parts to read unfamiliar words.**
☐ **I can use context clues or reread to correctly read and understand unfamiliar words.**

Read the passage. Then, read the poems aloud to another person.

Night Poetry

Robert Louis Stevenson (1850-1894) wrote the timeless adventure books *Kidnapped* and *Treasure Island*. Published in 1885, Stevenson's **collection** of poems, *A Child's Garden of Verses*, contains some of the best-known nighttime poetry written.

The Land of Nod

From breakfast on all through the day
At home among my friends I stay;
But every night I go **abroad**
Afar into the Land of Nod.

All by myself I have to go,
With none to tell me what to do—
All alone beside the streams
And up the mountain-sides of dreams.

The strangest things are there for me,
Both things to eat and things to see,
And many frightening sights abroad
Till morning in the Land of Nod.

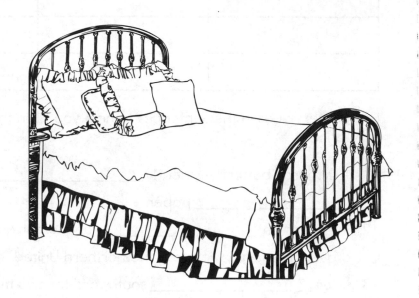

Try as I like to find the way,
I never can get back by day,
Nor can remember plain and clear
The **curious** music that I hear.

Shadow March (from "North-West Passage")

All round the house is the jet-black night;
It stares through the window-pane;
It crawls in the corners, hiding from the light,
And it moves with the moving flame.

Now my little heart goes a-beating like a drum,
With the breath of the **Bogies** in my hair;
And all round the candle the crooked shadows come,
And go marching along up the stair.

The shadows of the **balusters**, the shadow of the lamp,
The shadow of the child that goes to bed—
All the wicked shadows coming, tramp, tramp, tramp,
With the black night overhead.

☐ **I can read with accuracy, fluency, and expression.**

Use the passage and the poems on page 50 to answer the questions.

1. Write the simile in the second stanza of "Shadow March." _____

_____

2. Write a comparison of the sights and the music in "The Land of Nod." _____

_____

_____

3. What is the child doing in "The Land of Nod"?

    A. The child is playing.

    B. The child is eating.

    C. The child is dreaming.

4. What is the child afraid of in "Shadow March"? _____

_____

5. Name two things that the jet-black night does in "Shadow March." _____

_____

_____

6. How old was Robert Louis Stevenson when *A Child's Garden of Verses* was published?

_____

Write the letter of the synonym on the line next to its matching word. Use a dictionary for help.

7. _____ balusters   A. odd

8. _____ Bogies   B. set

9. _____ collection   C. pillars

10. _____ curious   D. away

11. _____ abroad   E. monsters

☐ **I can use context clues or reread to correctly read and understand unfamiliar words.**
☐ **I can use proper terms to explain the differences between poems, drama, and prose.**
☐ **I can explain what similes and metaphors mean in a text.**

Read the fables aloud to a classmate.

The Girl and the Almonds

A girl, hungry after a day of play, spied a jar of honeyed almonds sitting on the kitchen table. "Mom, may I please have some nuts?" she asked, her ravenous tummy growling.

"It's almost time for dinner," her mother said. "Only take a handful."

The greedy little girl reached into the jar, grabbing as many nuts as her fingers could hold. But when she tried to pull out her bulging hand, it got stuck in the narrow neck of the jar. Twisting and turning, she tugged until her arm grew sore and tears of disappointment flowed down her cheeks.

Amazed at her daughter's stubbornness, her mother said, "Let go of half the almonds, or you will end up with none at all."

Moral: A little at a time is better than none at all.

1. What does the moral mean? _____

_____

The Milkmaid and Her Pail

A young milkmaid was walking down a dusty path with a pail of fresh, warm cow's milk poised upon her head. As she neared her small, thatched-roof hut, daydreams filled her mind.

"The milk was so creamy this morning," she thought. "I'll churn the cream into golden butter that I will sell at the village market tomorrow. With the money I make from the butter I will buy a dozen eggs, and from the dozen eggs will hatch a dozen chickens. The dozen chickens will each lay a dozen eggs, and then I will have chickens, eggs, and butter to sell at the Autumn Fair.

"With the money I make at the fair I will buy a silver gown embroidered with pearls. This winter I will wear it to the Sheriff's Ball. When his son sees me, he'll seek me to dance. But will I? Oh, never! As he begs to take my hand, I'll sweetly smile and shake my head from side to side—like this!"

In that moment, the milkmaid's dreams turned back to reality. The wooden pail lay broken on the ground. In the end, she had nothing, not even the milk she started with.

Moral: Pay attention to the present so that the future might be what you dream.

2. What does the moral mean? _____

_____

☐ I can read with purpose.
☐ I can read with accuracy, fluency, and expression.
☐ I can read and comprehend grade-level fiction text.

Use the fables on page 52 to answer the questions.

1. What is the main idea of "The Girl and the Almonds"?

    A. Listen to what your mother says.

    B. Store nuts in a wide-mouthed jar.

    C. Do not be greedy.

2. What is the main idea of "The Milkmaid and Her Pail"?

    A. Check the sidewalk for rocks.

    B. Pay attention to what you are doing.

    C. Do not dream dreams.

3. What causes the milkmaid to drop the pail?

    A. She trips on the path.

    B. She shakes her head.

    C. She spills the milk.

4. What causes the girl's hand to get stuck in the jar?

    A. The neck of the jar is too wide.

    B. There are too many nuts in the jar.

    C. There are too many nuts in her hand.

5. Does the milkmaid like the sheriff's son? Write the sentence from the fable that supports

    your answer. _____

    _____

    _____

Write the base word of each word..

6. creamy _____

7. embroidered _____

8. stubbornness _____

9. honeyed _____

10. bulging _____

11. reality _____

12. dusty _____

13. wooden _____

14. twisting _____

15. turning _____

☐ I can use my knowledge of letter sounds, syllables, and word parts to read unfamiliar words.
☐ I can use details and examples in a text to explain and draw inferences.
☐ I can use details to determine the theme of a text.
☐ I can summarize the text.

Name_____

4.RF.4a, 4.RI.10

Sun and Water

Read the passage.

1   The Egyptians and Babylonians were fascinated with the sun and time. One of the earliest clocks was invented in the Middle East about 4,000 years ago. It is called a shadow clock. It was a T-shaped piece of wood with a time scale carved on it. As the sun rose into the sky, the shadow it cast became longer. After noon, as the day moved toward sunset, the shadow grew shorter.

2   A most inventive clock for cloudy days or indoor use was the water clock. The clepsydra (klep-sa-dra) had its origins, or beginnings, in Egypt about 1500 B.C. *Clepsydra* is a Greek word that means "water thief." Other night clocks, such as candle and rope clocks, could only be used once. The water clock could be used over and over again.

3   People have built water clocks for three millennia. Though the clocks were different, one basic rule remained the same. Water constantly dripped from one container through a small hole in its bottom to another. Perhaps the most famous use for this type of clock was in ancient Greece. There, lawyers'

speeches were limited by the number of drops that passed through the hole.

4   Egyptian clock makers formed clay pots with a tiny hole in the bottom and carved lines around the side. As water slowly dripped out of one pot into another, it was possible to tell how much time had passed by the changing water level.

5   In museums, you can see ancient water clocks that are glazed in beautiful colors with designs from the night sky. Some water clocks rang brass bells or opened wooden doors to reveal little dancing people.

6   Although sunlight wasn't needed for a water clock to work, it still had several problems. When it became very cold, the water would freeze and not drip at all. When it was very hot, the water would evaporate quickly. Eventually, the drip-drip of the water clock was replaced by the tick-tock of the mechanical clock. The first mechanical clock was built in the late fourteenth century.

☐ **I can read and comprehend grade-level informational text.**
☐ **I can read with purpose and understanding.**

54

© Carson-Dellosa • CD-104611

Find the word in the numbered paragraphs on page 54 that best fits the definition.

1. creative; original (2) _____

2. uses parts to create a complex tool (6) _____

3. one thousand years (3) _____

4. the people and culture of a certain African nation (4) _____

5. old; having had a long existence (5) _____

Write an antonym for each word.

6. fascinated _____

7. beginning _____

8. sunlight _____

9. melt _____

10. sunset _____

Write **F** before the sentences that are fact. Write **O** before the sentences that are opinion.

11. _____ The Egyptians were fascinated with the sun and time.

12. _____ Water clocks were glazed in beautiful colors.

13. _____ The word *clepsydra* means "water thief" in Greek.

14. _____ The water clock was a most inventive clock.

15. _____ Some water clocks rang brass bells.

☐ **I can comprehend while reading with accuracy and fluency.**
☐ **I can use context clues or reread to correctly read and understand unfamiliar words.**
☐ **I can use antonyms and synonyms to better understand words.**

Read the first three paragraphs. Then read all four limericks aloud to another person.

1   A limerick is a funny poem with five lines. In a limerick, lines 1, 2, and 5 rhyme, and lines 3 and 4 rhyme. We write this rhyme pattern **aabba**. The *a's* stand for lines 1, 2, and 5. The *b's* stand for lines 3 and 4. Where, when, and why people began to write limericks is unknown, but there are many possible answers.

2   One story says that the name *limerick* came from a form of song sung by Irish soldiers. They were returning to their hometown of Limerick after fighting a war in France in the early 1700s. Some say limericks appeared in ancient Greek plays centuries before then. William Shakespeare even wrote limericks in his plays. *Othello, King Lear*, and *Romeo and Juliet* all include limericks.

3   Edward Lear, an English poet, wrote an entire book of limericks. It was called *The Book of Nonsense* and was written in the nineteenth century. At that time, authors of children's books were not listed on the title page. It wasn't until many years later that Lear was recognized for his limericks. The first three limericks shown are by Edward Lear. The last one is by an unknown author.

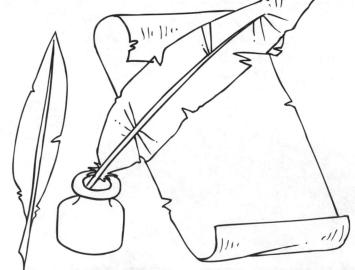

4   There was an Old Person of Tring

Who embellished his nose with a ring,

He gazed at the moon

Every evening in June,

The ecstatic Old person in Tring.

5   There was an Old Man who said, "Well!

Will nobody answer the bell?

I have pulled day and night,

Till my hair has grown white,

But nobody will answer this bell!"

6   There was an Old Man on whose nose,

Most birds of the air could repose.

But they all flew away,

At the close of the day,

Which relieved that Old Man and his nose.

7   There was a young lady named Bright,

Who traveled much faster than light.

She started one day

In a relative way,

And returned on the previous night.

☐ **I can read and comprehend grade-level informational text.**
☐ **I can read with purpose and understanding.**
☐ **I can read with accuracy, fluency, and expression.**

Find the word in the numbered paragraphs on page 56 that best fits the definition.

1. decorated (4) _____

2. to sleep; rest (6) _____

3. freed from pain or embarrassment (6) _____

4. not recognized as a fact or person (1) _____

5. a high state of happiness (4) _____

6. identify; know (3) _____

7. a famous English playwright (2) _____

8. Write the two homophones for *there*:

_____   _____

Follow the directions.

9. *Limericks* are silly, five-lined poems that rhyme in the following pattern: *aabba*. Write a limerick about time. Be sure to make it silly.

_____

_____

_____

_____

_____

10. Why was the Old Man relieved that the birds flew away at the end of the day?

_____

_____

11. Why do you think the names of children's book authors were not listed on title pages in the 1800s?

_____

_____

☐ **I can use my knowledge of letter sounds, syllables, and word parts to read unfamiliar words.**
☐ **I can use context clues or reread to correctly read and understand unfamiliar words.**

Read the passage.

The Scent of Night

Gourmet meals for moths and bats

1   A scent...an aroma...a smell—this is all a moth needs to find one of the many flowers that bloom as the sun sets. Unlike colorful butterflies or honeybees, the drab hawk moth and the little brown bat seek nectar at night.

2   Plants that flower by day need diurnal animals to help with pollination. Plants that bloom at night rely on nocturnal animals for the same reason. Pollen is a powdery substance inside flowers. Pollination occurs when pollen is moved from a flower on one plant to a flower on another plant. Without pollination, plants cannot make seeds for the next year. Most brightly colored flowers close their petals at night to keep their pollen dry. In the morning, after the night's dew has evaporated, the petals reopen. They are ready again for visits from tiny insects and birds.

   Take a visit to a garden at sunset. If you are lucky, you might see a daytime bug that has been trapped in a flower as its petals closed. Don't worry. The bug will be snug until the next morning.

3   Night-blooming flowers come in shades of pale white, yellow, and pink. They lack the dazzling colors of day bloomers because animals are not attracted to them by sight. Animals find these flowers by smell. Their fragrance during the day is often faint or unnoticeable. At night, however, a single blossom can fill an entire garden with its scent.

Honeysuckle

4   This vine has trumpet-shaped flowers and grows wild all over the world. Its creamy white and yellow blossoms make a gourmet meal for the hawk moth. Like the butterfly, this moth has a long proboscis that is perfect for sipping the flower's honey-flavored nectar.

5   If you have a honeysuckle plant near your house, visit it on a warm, moonlit night. Carefully remove a blossom by pinching off the slender stem at the bottom of the flower. With your fingernail, nip the green base of the flower in half. Gently pull back on the base until you see a drop of liquid. This is the flower's nectar.

Wild Banana Flower

6   Most night-flowering plants are pleasant for humans to smell. But there are some you just don't want to get near. The purple/brownish flower of the wild banana has rust-colored pollen. By its second day of blooming, it has a scent that reminds people of rotting meat. Silky brown bats are so attracted to this smell that they sometimes get trapped inside the flower's huge, stinky petals when they close at sunrise. What a way to spend the day!

☐ I can read and comprehend grade-level informational text.
☐ I can read with purpose and knowledge.

1. The wild banana flower stinks. What is the effect? _____

_____.

2. Do nocturnal or diurnal animals pollinate night-blooming plants? _____

_____

3. Why are night-blooming plants so pale?

_____

_____

4. What helps the hawk moth get nectar out of the honeysuckle flower? _____

_____

5. Why do you think day-blooming plants need to keep their pollen dry? (Hint" Think of how the powdery pollen is transported.)

_____

_____

6. The author has two opinions in paragraph 6.

Write one of them. _____

Write the number of the word in front of its definition. Use a dictionary if you need help.

7. _____ drab   A. special, tasty

8. _____ dew   B. to look for something

9. _____ stinky   C. a reddish-brown color

10. _____ evaporate   D. drops of water

11. _____ fragrance   E. to clip or snip

12. _____ seek   F. to dry up

13. _____ rely   G. to be smelly

14. _____ gourmet   H. scent; aroma

15. _____ nip   I. colorless

16. _____ rust   J. to depend on

17. If the suffix *re-* means "do again," what does reopen mean?

_____

18. If the suffix *un-* means "not," what does the word *unnoticeable* mean?

_____

19. Write three compound words in paragraph 5 on page 58.

_____ _____ _____

20. Write the two compound words in paragraph 1 on page 58.

_____ _____

☐ **I can use my knowledge of letter sounds, syllables, and word parts to read unfamiliar words.**

☐ **I can use context clues or reread to correctly read and understand unfamiliar words.**

Do you remember the first time that you rode a bike or the first time that you rode on a roller coaster? Fill in the web with examples of your experiences. These examples can lead to great stories.

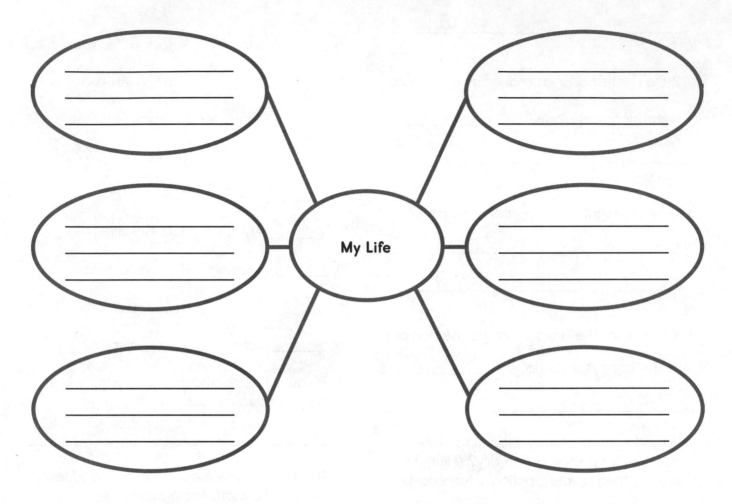

Look at the examples that you wrote on the web. List three experiences that you can write about.

1. _____

2. _____

3. _____

☐ **I can establish a situation in a story.**

60

Many students love the summer. Think about the summer and why this time of year is special. Complete the chart with examples and details that support the two reasons.

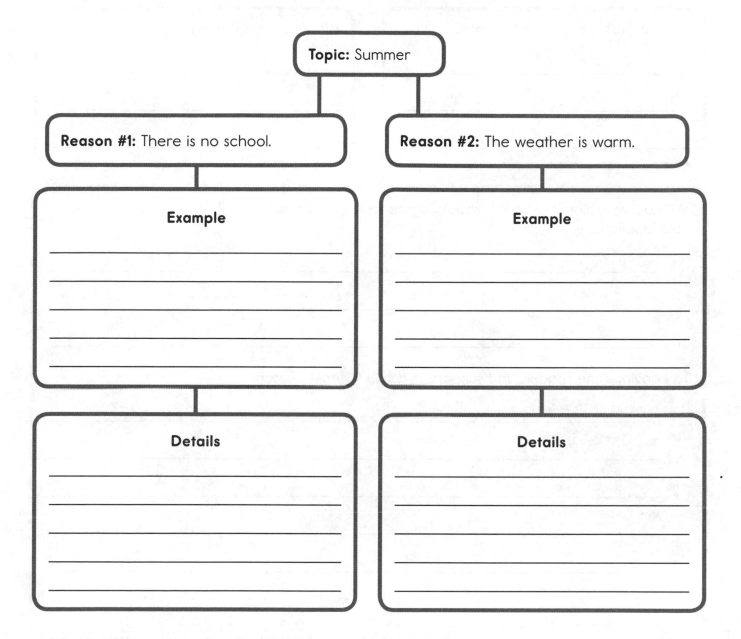

Topic: Summer

Reason #1: There is no school.

Reason #2: The weather is warm.

Example

_____
_____
_____
_____

Example

_____
_____
_____
_____

Details

_____
_____
_____
_____

Details

_____
_____
_____
_____

☐ I can organize my writing and use text features to help readers better understand a topic.
☐ I can use specific information like facts, definitions, and details to support a topic.

Choose a topic. Use the graphic organizer to help you plan a persuasive essay.

What is your opinion on the topic?

_____

_____

_____

Whom are you trying to persuade?

_____

_____

_____

Why do you think that others should agree with your opinion? List three reasons to support your opinion.

1. _____

2. _____

3. _____

To convince the reader, add supporting details for each reason.

1. _____

_____

2. _____

_____

3. _____

_____

On another piece of paper, use your notes to help you write a five-paragraph persuasive essay. Include three reasons, in addition to introductory and concluding paragraphs. Use linking words and phrases such as *for instance, in order to, in addition,* and *as well as.*

☐ I can organize my writing to support an opinion.
☐ I can use facts and details to support reasons.
☐ I can use words and phrases to connect an opinion and reasons.

Name_____

Imagine that your teacher has decided to rearrange students' desks. Should students be allowed to choose where they sit in class? Use the graphic organizer to help you plan your persuasive paragraph.

What is your opinion on the topic?

_____

_____

_____

Whom are you trying to persuade?

_____

_____

_____

Why do you think that others should agree with your opinion? List three reasons to support your opinion.

1. _____

_____

2. _____

_____

3. _____

_____

Use your notes to help you write a five-sentence persuasive paragraph. Include a closing statement that restates your opinion.

_____

_____

_____

_____

☐ I can organize my writing to support an opinion.
☐ I can use facts and details to support reasons.
☐ I can use words and phrases to connect an opinion and reasons.

Imagine that someone has asked you for the directions to make your favorite sandwich. Help them by writing the steps. Use at least six time-order words. Examples are given in the word bank.

eventually	last	shortly after
finally	next	soon
first	now	then

How to Make My Favorite _____ Sandwich

_____

_____

_____

_____

_____

_____

_____

_____

_____

_____

_____

_____

_____

_____

_____

☐ I can use words and phrases to connect an opinion and reasons.

Think about a time when you or someone you know found something unexpected. Write a terrific beginning for your story using action or dialogue. Use words from the word bank to help.

amazed	confused	demanded
discovered	exclaimed	explored
gasped	investigated	replied

_____

_____

_____

_____

_____

_____

_____

_____

_____

_____

_____

_____

_____

_____

_____

☐ I can write a conclusion related to an opinion.
☐ I can gather information, take and organize notes, and provide resources.
☐ I can write over different time periods for various purposes and audiences.

Imagine that you woke up one morning and were 10 feet (3 meters) tall. What would you do if you were that tall? Write a terrific beginning for your story using onomatopoeia (sound words) or the five senses (hearing, sight, touch, taste, and smell). Use words from the word bank to help.

Onomatopoeia Word Bank	Five Senses Word Bank
bang	appeared
honk	looked
screech	saw
crash	felt
giggle	heard
sigh	touched

_____

_____

_____

_____

_____

_____

_____

_____

_____

_____

_____

_____

_____

☐ I can use specific words related to the topic to support my writing.
☐ I can use descriptive words and details to help readers better understand a story.
☐ I can write over different time periods for various purposes and audiences.

A good friend is someone whom you can count on. But, even best friends can have disagreements. Imagine that you are writing a story about two friends who have a disagreement. Use the chart to list the main events in the beginning, middle, and end of your story.

Beginning

_____

_____

_____

_____

Middle

_____

_____

_____

_____

End

_____

_____

_____

_____

☐ I can establish a situation, introduce characters and a narrator, and organize events in a story.

☐ I can write a conclusion that completes a story.

Good stories have good endings.

Read the story details. Write a satisfying ending to the story by asking a question or having the characters learn a lesson.

Characters
Scotty is a golden retriever who loves to play fetch.
Mark is Scotty's owner.

Problem
Scotty gets lost in the park while playing fetch with Mark.

Solution
Mark finally finds Scotty waiting for him by the swings.

Satisfying Ending

_____

_____

_____

_____

_____

_____

_____

_____

_____

_____

_____

☐ **I can establish a situation, introduce characters and a narrator, and organize events in a story.**
☐ **I can write a conclusion that completes a story.**

Read "The Crow Who Brought the Daylight" on page 24. Use the flowchart to help you recognize the strategies the author of this story used.

Setting: _____

Characters: _____

Problem: _____

Event 1: _____
_____
_____
_____
_____
_____
_____

Event 2: _____
_____
_____
_____
_____
_____
_____

Event 3: _____
_____
_____
_____
_____
_____
_____

Solution: _____

Using this information, write a five-sentence paragraph that tells about the story.

_____

_____

_____

_____

_____

☐ **I can use grade-level reading strategies when writing about fiction texts.**

Name_____

Read "Food for Survival" on page 35. Use the flowchart to help you recognize the strategies the author of this story used.

Setting: _____

↓

Characters: _____

↓

Problem: _____

Event 1: _____	Event 2: _____	Event 3: _____
_____	_____	_____
_____	_____	_____
_____	_____	_____
_____	_____	_____
_____	_____	_____

Solution: _____

Using this information, write a five-sentence paragraph that tells about the story.

_____

_____

_____

_____

_____

☐ **I can use grade-level reading strategies when writing about informational texts.**

Name_____

Choose a topic. Research it carefully using books, the Internet, and encyclopedias. Fill out the graphic organizer. Then, use the information to write a paragraph about your topic.

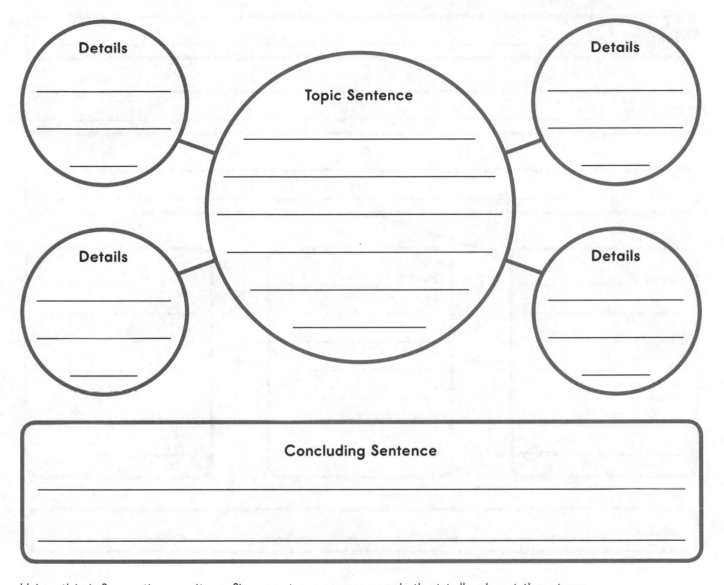

Details

_____

_____

Topic Sentence

_____

_____

_____

_____

_____

Details

_____

_____

Details

_____

_____

Details

_____

_____

Concluding Sentence

_____

_____

Using this information, write a five-sentence paragraph that tells about the story.

_____

_____

_____

_____

☐ I can consider the purpose and the audience when writing.
☐ I can research different aspects of a topic.
☐ I can write over different time periods for various purposes and audiences.

Write a story that tells about your favorite childhood memory. Include dialogue as you remember it. Use the flowchart to help you plan your story.

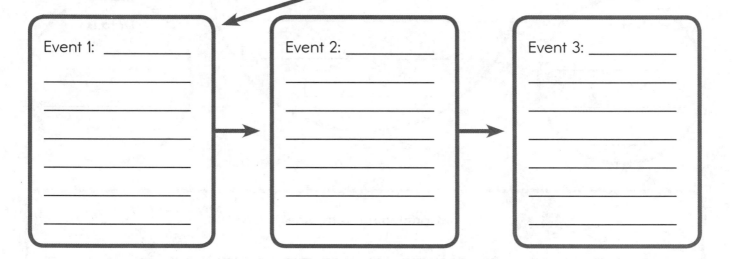

Setting: _____

Characters: _____

Problem: _____

Event 1: _____

_____

_____

_____

_____

_____

Event 2: _____

_____

_____

_____

_____

_____

Event 3: _____

_____

_____

_____

_____

_____

Solution: _____

Using this information, write a five-sentence paragraph that tells about the story.

_____

_____

_____

_____

☐ **I can establish a situation, introduce characters and a narrator, and organize events in a story.**
☐ **I can use dialogue and descriptions to enhance events and characters in a story.**

Use the editing checklist to produce a final copy of your narrative story written on page 72. Type your final draft on the computer or write it on another sheet of paper. Attach your first draft along with this editing sheet to your final draft before turning it in.

Plan

_____ I have made a written plan that outlines the setting, characters, events, and conclusion of my story.

Revise

_____ I have written an interesting start to my story that catches the reader's attention.

_____ I have written a closing that effectively ends my story.

_____ I have revised my writing for vivid and descriptive words.

_____ I used transition words and phrases to connect my writing.

Edit

_____ I used words correctly.

_____ I have written complete sentences.

_____ I have edited my writing for correct capitalization and punctuation.

_____ I have edited my writing for spelling errors.

Publish

_____ I have decided how I will publish and share my writing.

© Carson-Dellosa • CD-104611

☐ I can plan, revise, and edit my writing.
☐ I can use technology resources to create, publish, and share my writing.
☐ I can write over different time periods for various purposes and audiences.

Follow the directions to write an informative essay.

1. Choose a significant current event. Research the topic using the Internet, an encyclopedia, or other books. Make notes about the topic in the table.

Topic: _____

Introduction: _____

_____

Body: _____

_____

_____

_____

Conclusion: _____

_____

2. Include vocabulary that a reader must know to understand your topic. Write at least three important words and their definitions.

_____

_____

_____

3. Use words and phrases to link ideas, such as *above all, actually, also, another, as well as, for example, because, in addition to, in conclusion, last but not least, to begin with.*

4. Use this information to write a first draft of your essay on another sheet of paper.

5. Include an illustration of a main event from your topic.

☐ **I can use words and phrases to connect ideas within sections.**
☐ **I can use specific words related to the topic to support my writing.**
☐ **I can write a conclusion related to the topic.**

Use this checklist to analyze the first draft of your current events essay began on page 74. Note any necessary changes on your first draft. Then, type your final draft on the computer or write it on another sheet of paper. Keep your first and final drafts together.

_____ My essay has a main topic.

_____ My essay is about a significant current event.

_____ I have included essential facts and details.

_____ I have listed details that support the main idea.

_____ I have used vocabulary that fits the topic.

_____ I have given my essay an interesting title.

_____ My essay has an introduction, a body, and a conclusion.

_____ The sentences are complete sentences.

_____ I have used an interesting mix of vocabulary, including active verbs and descriptive adjectives and adverbs.

_____ I have used proper punctuation where needed.

_____ I have checked that all of the words are spelled correctly.

_____ I have capitalized all proper words.

☐ I can plan, revise, and edit my writing.
☐ I can use technology resources to create, publish, and share my writing.
☐ I can write over different time periods for various purposes and audiences.

Fill in the blanks using a relative pronoun from the word bank.

that	whichever	whoever	whomever
which	who	whom	whose

1. This is the new bicycle _____ I bought with my allowance.

2. The drama coach chose students _____ he thought were the best actors.

3. I want to ride with _____ is the best driver.

4. _____ student got the best grades would pass out the awards.

5. _____ finishes their dinner can have dessert.

6. My neighbor, _____ cat won't come down, is understandably upset.

7. The pot roast, _____ was left out overnight, should be thrown out.

8. The person _____ has the latest birthday will go first.

Fill in the blank using a relative adverb from the word bank. One of them will be used twice.

where	when	why

9. That is the school _____ I first met you.

10. It was a very hot day _____ Jose went swimming for the first time.

11. Tell me _____ you can't make it for practice.

12. Kelly will hand it in _____ she has answered all the questions.

☐ **I can use relative pronouns and adverbs.**

Write the progressive tense of each verb. (Example: *was walking, am walking, will be walking*)

	past progressive	present progressive	future progressive
1. write	_____	_____	_____
2. swim	_____	_____	_____
3. read	_____	_____	_____
4. play	_____	_____	_____
5. eat	_____	_____	_____
6. sit	_____	_____	_____

Complete each sentence with the correct progressive tense of each verb in parentheses.

7. I _____ soccer after school right now. (play)

8. Next fall, I _____ a different sport. (play)

9. In first grade, I _____ much easier sports. (play)

Circle the best modal auxiliary verb to complete the sentence.

10. I (can, could) play "Old MacDonald" on the piano already.

11. The senator (may, might) become president in two years.

12. She (must, has to) clean her room before she can go to the mall.

13. I (shall, should) eat a salad for lunch.

14. The team (will, would) win always the game when they played well.

☐ **I can form and use progressive verbs.**
☐ **I can use helping verbs such as *can, may,* and *must* to express time and mood.**

Use the nouns and verbs to write sentences with complete subjects and complete predicates.

1. car   roar

_____

2. birds   flock

_____

3. helmets   ride

_____

4. students   run

_____

5. glasses   break

_____

Draw a box around each complete subject. Circle each complete predicate. Underline any sentence fragments. Rewrite each fragment as a complete sentence.

6. The gentle manatee lives in shallow water. _____

7. Sometimes called sea cows. _____

8. Most West Indian manatees live in Florida. _____

9. They look for food at the water's surface. _____

10. A resting manatee. _____

11. The average adult manatee is three meters (9.8 feet) long. _____

12. Manatees eat all types of plants. _____

☐ **I can form complete sentences and correct fragments and run-on sentences.**

Write the pair of adjectives in the correct order.

1. The dog is a _____, _____ Labrador retriever. (black, big)

2. I am going to bake a _____, _____ cake.
   (chocolate, delicious)

3. Please recycle the _____, _____ water bottles. (empty, six)

4. Robert is wearing a _____, _____ coat. (green, long)

5. She gave Tanisha some _____, _____ clothes. (pretty, new)

Underline the prepositional phrase in each sentence.

6. The dime fell between the cracks.

7. The money for my lunch is missing.

8. Juan fell on the steps and hurt himself.

9. Miss Gomez was visiting our school from a nearby college.

10. Mrs. Chang wrote a note about my behavior.

Choose the correct word from the list to complete each sentence.

11. _____ going to be the best one of _____ kind. (it's, its)

12. I stopped _____ the store to _____ some milk. (by, buy)

13. The _____ beat the tortoise by a _____. (hair, hare)

14. Marta went _____ the store today. Abby was there _____.

    So, the _____ girls shopped together. (to, too, two)

15. I heard _____ are going to be at least 100 people at

    _____ wedding. My neighbors said that _____ going to be

    there too. (there, they're, their)

☐ **I can use adjectives in the correct order in a sentence.**
☐ **I can form and use prepositional phrases.**
☐ **I can correctly use frequently confused words such as *to, too,* and *two*.**

Rewrite these sentences using correct capitalization and punctuation.

1. can we please stay for 10 more minutes the children asked

_____

2. i knew about the surprise party all along jonah admitted

_____

3. that was a really silly joke alyssa giggled

_____

4. I think i have a cold so dont get too close maggie warned

_____

5. shh she might hear us liz whispered

_____

6. i didnt mean to do it but I couldn't help myself serena confessed

_____

7. you can do it the coach cheered

_____

8. first line up all of the numbers and then add them the teacher explained.

_____

9. the water in the pool is chilly today the lifeguard warned

_____

10. stir the ingredients well the cooking instructor suggested

_____

☐ I can correctly capitalize words.
☐ I can use correct punctuation when writing quotations and dialogue.
☐ I can use a comma before a coordinating conjunction in a compound sentence.

Rewrite the sentences. Add quotations marks and capital letters where needed.

1. i thought about taking a bus, but I finally decided to take an airplane, Emily said.

_____

_____

2. i am not sure, tony sighed. i just can't remember where i left my keys. _____

_____

_____

3. the treasure is hidden in the forest, the prince whispered. _____

_____

4. did you see where melinda went? tyler asked. i want to invite her over for lunch.

_____

_____

5. sue asked, do you know how to grow an herb garden? _____

_____

6. i want to learn to play the cello, maria said. will you teach me? _____

_____

7. jelly beans are my favorite! Daniel shouted. i love the cherry-flavored ones.

_____

_____

☐ **I can correctly capitalize words.**
☐ **I can use correct punctuation when writing quotations and dialogue.**

Read the story. Cross out each word that is misspelled. Then write the correct spellings on the lines below. Use a dictionary if you need it.

Stained Glass

Alexis and Emma had to write a report for werld history. They were studying the Middle Ages. Some of the boys were writing reports about nights, the Black Death, and the Krusades. Some of the girls were writing reports about tapestries, costumes, and liturature.

Alexis and Emma wanted to do something different. They met one Saturday at the library. They used the catolog on the computer to find books about the Middle Ages.

They found many subjects listed under Middle Ages. Alexis pointed to Gothic Cathedral. "Just last month, I saw a documentary about building a cathedral," she said. "Everybody in the town helped. Some men started working on the cathedral when they were yung. They worked on it their whole lives."

"That was a book too," said Emma. "I read it last year. Let's find the books on cathedrals."

The two girls printed out the list of books. Then, they found the write sektion in the library. Two of the books were checked out, but the other for were on the shelf. Alexis took two, and Emma took two.

They went to a quiet table and started to look at the pictures. Alexis found a picture of a beutiful stained glass window.

She read that the cathedrals were made of stone. They were also very tall. They needed big windows to bring light into the building. The artists desined windows made of pieces of colorful glass. When light came through the windows, people inside the cathedral could see glowing pictures or designs.

Alexis showed Emma the picture. They decided to write their report on staned glass windows in cathedrals.

1. _____   2. _____

3. _____   4. _____

5. _____   6. _____

7. _____   8. _____

9. _____   10. _____

11. _____ 12. _____

☐ I can spell words correctly.
☐ I can refer to sources when I need help spelling a word.

Write a sentence to convey the emotion in parentheses.

1. (happiness) _____

_____

2. (excitement) _____

_____

3. (sorrow) _____

_____

4. (disappointment) _____

_____

5. (surprise) _____

_____

Look at each pair of sentences. Place an **S** for *slang* or a **P** for *proper English* in front of each.

6. _____ Let's call it a day, man.

_____ Let's stop working now.

7. _____ That race was quite easy for me.

_____ That race was a piece of cake, bro.

8. _____ Hang in there.

_____ Keep trying.

9. _____ Tell my friends I said hello.

_____ Say hey to my peeps for me.

10. _____ C'mon, take a load off.

_____ Take it easy.

☐ **I can choose words and phrases that best express my ideas.**
☐ **I can choose to use formal or informal language in different situations.**

Put a question mark at the end of each interrogative sentence. Put an exclamation point at the end of each exclamatory sentence.

1. Do you know how many teeth an adult human has

2. Does he or she have 32 teeth

3. Did you realize that zebras have teeth like rats

4. Hey! You must be kidding

5. Wow! Zebras grind down their teeth by eating 15 hours a day

6. Can their teeth just keep growing like rodents' teeth

7. That is amazing

8. Is it true that great white sharks have razor-sharp teeth

Rewrite each sentence and add the correct ending punctuation mark. Then, read them aloud to another person with the proper emphasis.

9. You will not believe this

_____

10. What are you talking about

_____

11. Wow! A snail has teeth on its tongue

_____

12. Goodness! There are thousands of tiny teeth

_____

☐ **I can use punctuation to affect meaning in my writing.**

4.L.4a, 4.RL.10

Read the story.

King Arthur

Legend says that England once had a **noble** king named Arthur who fought for good and **respectable** things. There are many stories from the Middle Ages in which King Arthur is the hero. He **defeated** his foes and won the love and admiration of his countrymen.

King Arthur held his court in a place called Camelot, and his knights sat at a round table. The symbolic round table showed that they all worked together and that no one was at the head of the table. In King Arthur's court, no knight had more responsibility or **influence** than any other knight. King Arthur is said to have brought order and peace to his kingdom.

As a child, Arthur discovered his **regal** legacy when he was the only person who could free a sword that was **lodged** in a stone outside a cathedral. Arthur's father and mother died when he was young, and he was raised by his uncle.

With the help of a magician, Merlin, he was guided to his destiny. He later married the beautiful Guinevere, whom he loved deeply. He and his knights were known for their kindness, gentleness, and chivalry. He received his famous sword, Excalibur, as a gift from the "Lady of the Lake." This was the sword that he used in battle many times. Some **legends** say that King Arthur died on the Isle of Avalon. Others say that Arthur will return one day.

Based on the context of each bold word, write a brief definition.

1. _____

2. _____

3. _____

4. _____

5. _____

6. _____

7. _____

☐ I can use context clues to understand an unfamiliar word or phrase.
☐ I can read and comprehend grade-level fiction text.

Name_____

Complete each simile.

1. as stubborn as _____

2. as clumsy as _____

3. as loud as _____

Write a sentence using each simile that you created.

4. _____

5. _____

6. _____

Read the metaphors. Write a sentence explaining the meaning of each metaphor.

Example: He clammed up when his parents asked him who broke the vase.
        This means that he kept his mouth closed when his parents questioned him.

7. The stars were jewels in the night sky. _____

_____

8. Jessica is a treasure chest of ideas. _____

_____

9. My mind was a sponge soaking up all of her brilliant ideas. _____

_____

10. The field wore a coat of gold. _____

_____

☐ **I can explain what similes and metaphors mean in a text.**

Name_____

Read the idioms. Explain what you think each one means.

1. Piece of cake: _____

2. Tongue-tied: _____

3. Over-the-hill: _____

4. Hit the sack: _____

5. All ears: _____

Write a sentence using each idiom.

6. Cat got your tongue: _____

_____

7. See eye to eye: _____

_____

8. Toot your own horn: _____

_____

9. Raining cats and dogs: _____

_____

10. A piece of cake: _____

_____

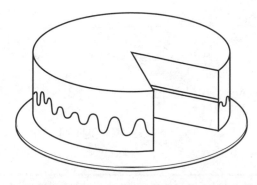

☐ **I can recognize and explain idioms, adages, and proverbs.**

Identify whether each sentence includes a simile or a metaphor. Write **S** if the sentence includes a simile. Write **M** is the sentence includes a metaphor.

1. _____ The ocean is a hungry animal.

2. _____ Her expression was as sour as a lime.

3. _____ I dried the dishes so well that they sparkled like diamonds.

4. _____ My room is a junkyard.

5. _____ Gavin's compliment made my face turn red as an apple.

Describe your best friend. Write one sentence using a simile and one sentence using a metaphor.

6. Simile: _____

7. Metaphor: _____

These statements contain idioms. Read the sentences. Circle the answers that give the correct meanings of the idioms.

8. Alice had butterflies in her stomach before the tennis match.

    A. was coming down with the flu   B. was nervous

9. Tell me about it. I'm all ears.

    A. listening carefully   B. covered in ears

10. That noise is driving me up the wall.

    A. bothering me   B. very loud

11. Hold your horses. I am coming!

    A. stop running   B. wait patiently

12. This puzzle is difficult. I'm in over my head.

    A. in deep water   B. struggling

☐ **I can explain what similes and metaphors mean in a text.**
☐ **I can recognize and explain idioms, adages, and proverbs.**

Imagine a beetle so bright that humans used it instead of a candle at night. The cucujo beetle found in Central America is that bug. Native people long ago would tie cucujos to their feet to light their way along steep mountain paths. During summer festivals, young girls would decorate their hair with this glowing beetle.

The light is produced from a chemical reaction called **bioluminescence** (bi/o/loom/in/es/since). There are insects, fish, and even some plants that produce this light.

Fireflies, or lightning bugs, are found in the eastern United States. (Fireflies are not actually flies. They're beetles.) They are seen on warm evenings in early summer. This beetle is the only insect that can flash its light on and off. The male flashes a pattern of light to females resting on the ground. Think of it as the firefly's way of asking for a date. Sometimes frogs eat so many fireflies that they start to glow from the inside out.

In the Pacific and Indian Oceans and the Red Sea, flashlight fish live among coral reefs. As the sun sets, they rise to the surface. Smaller fish attracted by the light become easy **prey**. There is no creature that gives off a brighter light. In fact, fishermen can see the light over 100 feet away!

The light is caused by **bacteria**. The bacteria grow in patches below the fish's eyes and give off a blue-green glow. When trying to avoid a **predator**, the flashlight fish constantly changes directions as it swims away. To confuse its attacker, it blinks its light on and off. It does this by slipping a cover, like an eyelid, over the shining patches.

Other night creatures that glow in the dark are anchovies, jellyfish, squid, some earthworms, and the railroad worm. A fungus or mushroom called the yellow jack-o'-lantern produces a bright greenish light. But don't eat it—it's **poisonous**.

Use each word in a sentence. Consult a dictionary if you need help.

1. bioluminescence _____

2. prey _____

3. bacteria _____

4. predator _____

5. poisonous _____

☐ **I can learn and use academic and subject-specific vocabulary.**
☐ **I can read and comprehend grade-level informational text.**

Write the word that is the antonym of the other words. Use a dictionary if needed.

1. young   early   old   juvenile _____

2. cold   hot   chilly   freezing _____

3. dirty   clean   sterile   immaculate _____

4. flop   fail   win   lose _____

5. fling   throw   toss   catch _____

6. sluggish   fast   slow   leisurely _____

7. grand   impressive   magnificent   humble _____

8. neat   orderly   sloppy   tidy _____

Circle the synonym in parentheses for each bold word in the sentences.

9. My mother was surprised when she saw the **beautiful** flowers. (pretty, red)

10. The librarian asked Maria to be **silent** because her classmates were trying to study. (cheerful, quiet)

11. My brother rode a **miniature** pony on his birthday. (pretty, small)

12. The judge made a **wise** decision about the case. (funny, intelligent)

13. Sam's grandfather is too **elderly** to walk that far. (old, interesting)

14. Adele's parents will enjoy their 20th anniversary **celebration**. (party, parade)

15. Aren't you **exhausted** after your long race? (hungry, tired)

16. Algebra problems are **difficult** for many kids. (hard, easy)

☐ I can use reference materials to learn about unfamiliar words and phrases.
☐ I can use antonyms and synonyms to better understand words.

Answer Key

Page 12
1. B; 2. A; 3. A; 4. B

Page 13
1. to be in a warm climate;
2. going camping; 3. often had afternoon showers; 4. for a long weekend; 5. in the woods; 6. in a lake; 7. not too far from home; 8. brought back fish

Page 14
1–3. Answers will vary.

Page 15
1. A; 2. B; 3. C; 4–6. Answers will vary.

Page 16.
1–6. Drawings will vary.

Page 17
1. She prefers to be alone.
2. Answers will vary. 3. Answers will vary but may include observant, kind, thoughtful, heroic

Page 18
1. first person, author; 2. third person, Tony and Jose; 3. third person, Erin

Page 19
1. Astronomy; 2. especially;
3. planetarium; 4. telescope;
5. conditions; 6. observations;
7. constellations; 8. over;
9. compass; 10. expedition

Page 21
1. 3, 1, 2, 4; 2. 40 years old;
3. Answers will vary but may include Bill doesn't grow much older, while Bob gets 20 years older. 4. past; 5. sea; 6. thyme;
7. cry; 8. carrot; 9. awesome;
10. idea; 11. relative; 12. different;
13. study; 14. fast

Page 23
1–6. Answers will vary. 7. mid and night, street and car; 8. bare and foot; 9. a kind of fruit; 10. a period of not eating food; 11. to grow old; 12. put up with

Page 25
1-5. Answers will vary; 6. The Inuit live in the Arctic regions of the US, Canada, Greenland, and Siberia.

Page 26
1. Friendly; 2. eleven; 3. sweet;
4. rabbit; 5. beagle; 6. Travers;
7. Becky; 8. mean; 9. Preston;
10. Sunday; 11. Marty; 12. Shiloh;
The book received the Newbery Medal.

Page 27
1. Answers will vary but should include that the dogs were strays, that their new owners eventually loved them. 2. Marty found his dog by the river; Old Yeller showed up on Travis's farm.
3. Answers will vary.

Page 28
1. Long ago, festivals were held when there was a good harvest.
2. The first European settlers in America had a fall festival that they named Thanksgiving.
3. There is usually a celebration of some sort after a harvest.

Page 29
1. Ancient civilizations did not have scientific information that explained the causes of earthquakes. 2. Some Native Americans thought a giant sea turtle held up Earth. 3. In India, it was believed that four elephants held up Earth. 4. The ancient Greeks thought earthquakes showed the gods' anger.

Page 30
1. C; 2. C; 3. B

Page 31

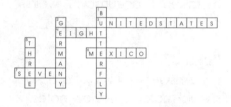

Page 32

Gastropods	Bivalves	Chitons
single, coiled shells	two shells hinged together at one end or along one side	8 shell plates that look like a turtle's shell
beaches of the Atlantic and Pacific oceans in North America	coasts of the Atlantic and Pacific oceans in North America	shallow rock pools in Pacific Ocean from Alaska to Mexico
limpets, snails, slugs, whelks	clams, mussels, oysters, scallops	Merten's chiton, northern red chiton, mossy mopalia

Answer Key

Page 33
1. four; 2. Cenozoic, Mesozoic, Paleozoic, Precambrian; 3. Mesozoic; 4. three; 5. Cretaceous, Jurassic, Triassic 6. Cenozoic

Page 34
1. Asia; 2. Nile, Amazon; 3. Australia, Europe; 4. Australia; 5. Mount Everest, Mount McKinley, Aconcagua

Page 35
1. range; 2. incorporated; 3. natives; 4. contingent; 5. stalked; 6. accuracy; 7. weirs; 8. culture

Page 37
1–8. Answers will vary. Paragraph should match interview notes.

Page 38
1. J; 2. C 3. M; 4. L; 5. O; 6. F; 7. A; 8. N; 9. G; 10. B; 11. I; 12. K; 13. H; 14. E; 15. D

Page 39
Answers will vary.

Page 41
1. B; 2. A; 3. Calcium helps strengthen teeth. 4. Fluoride reduces the number of cavities. 5. The Importance of Dental Floss: removes accumulated plaque; William Addis: invented the toothbrush, used bone and hairbrush bristles; Tooth Cleaners Over the Years: scratched their teeth with sticks, wiped their teeth with rags, chewed on crushed bones or shells; Tooth Cleaning Today: fluoride toothpaste, dental floss, specially angled toothbrushes.

Page 43
1. Answers will vary. 2. The coast is rocky, and it has lighthouses. 3. Answers will vary. 4. Stevenson loved to travel and write. 5. *A Child's Garden of Verses;* 6. Answers will vary. 7. Answers will vary. 8. tourist; 9. Europe; 10. popcorn; 11. playmate; 12. nights; 13. terrible; 14. worst; 15. poor

Page 45
1. No one had studied the sky with a telescope until Galileo in the sixteenth century. 2. jeudi; 3. the sun, the moon, Mars, Mercury, Jupiter, Venus, and Saturn; 4. Saturn; 5. Friday's child is loving and giving. 6. C; 7. E; 8. A; 9. D; 10. B; 11. The year was broken into weeks. 12. Some days were named after Nordic and Anglo-Saxon gods.

Page 47
1. C; 2. B; 3. B; 4. B; 5. C; 6. A; 7. E; 8. B; 9. F; 10. D

Page 48
1. D, f; 2. J, a; 3. K, b; 4. I, g; 5. E, d; 6. G or L, e; 7. B, k; 8. A, h; 9. H, j; 10. C, c; 11. F, l; 12. G or L, i

Page 49
1 syllable: hatch, jaws, mate; 2 syllables: tissue, nectar, soaring; 3 syllables: tansparent, finally, bothersome; 4 syllables: migratory, caterpillars, honeysuckle

1. transparent, tissue; 2. nectar, migratory; 3. soaring, finally; 4. mate; 5. caterpillars, hatch; 6. jaws; 7. bothersome; 8. honeysuckle

Page 51
1. Now my little heart goes a-beating like a drum; 2. Answers will vary. 3. C; 4. The child is afraid of the dark. 5. Answers will vary. 6. Stevenson was 35 years old. 7. C; 8. E; 9. B; 10. A; 11. D

Page 52
1. Answers will vary. 2. Answers will vary.

Page 53
1. C; 2. B; 3. B; 4. C; 5. No. As he begs to take my hand, I'll smile sweetly and shake my head from side to side. 6. cream; 7. embroider; 8. stubborn; 9. honey; 10. bulge; 11. real; 12. dust; 13. wood; 14. twist; 15. turn

Page 55
1. inventive; 2. mechanical; 3. millennia; 4. Egyptian; 5. ancient; 6. bored; 7. end; 8. moonlight/dark; 9. freeze; 10. sunrise; 11. O; 12. O; 13. F; 14. O; 15. F

Page 57
1. embellished; 2. repose; 3. relieved; 4. unknown; 5. ecstatic; 6. recognized; 7. William Shakespeare; 8. their, they're; 9. Answers will vary. 10. because the birds sat on his nose; 11. Answers will vary.

Answer Key

Page 59
1. The silky brown bat is attracted to it. 2. nocturnal animals; 3. They don't need any color because they attract by smell, not sight. 4. its proboscis; 5. If the pollen was wet, it would be in a clump and wouldn't stick. 6. 1. What a way to spend a day! 2. There are some you just don't want to get near. 7. I; 8. D; 9. G; 10. F; 11. H; 12. B; 13. J; 14. A; 15. E; 16; C; 17. open again; 18. not noticeable; 19. honeysuckle, moonlit, fingernail; 20. butterflies, honeybees

Page 60
1–3. Answers will vary but should be experiences listed on their web.

Page 61
Examples and details will vary.

Page 62
Answers will vary.

Page 63
Answers will vary.

Page 64
Essays will vary but must include at least six time-order words.

Page 65
Essays will vary but must include some words from the Action and Dialogue Word Bank.

Page 66
Story beginnings will vary but should include some words from the Onomatopoeia and Five Senses Word Banks.

Page 67
Essays will vary.

Page 68
Paragraphs will vary but should include a satisfying ending.

Page 69
Setting: Inuit land in the north; Characters: Crow, Inuit people, village girl and her father and brother; Problem: Inuits lived in darkness; Event 1: Inuit people heard about daylight; Event 2: Crow flew east to find daylight; Event 3: Crow stole a ball of daylight; Solution: Crow brought daylight back to the Inuit people. Paragraphs will vary but should retell the story in the correct sequence.

Page 70
Setting: northern forests in North America; Characters: Native Americans; Problem: The rocky land was not good for farming; Event 1: Native Americans learned how to be good hunters; Event 2: They stalked and hunted moose and caribou; Event 3: They used weirs, nets, traps, hooks, and spears to catch other food; Solution: Because they learned to hunt, they had plenty to eat.

Page 71
Paragraphs will vary but should be five sentences long and include the topic sentence and surrounding details from the graphic organizer.

Page 72
Stories will vary but should include dialogue.

Page 74
1. Accept any appropriate topic. Notes should include significant facts and details. 2. The list should include three or more words and definitions that pertain to the topic. 3. Observe use of some of the suggested linking words. 4. Essays will vary. 5. Illustrations will vary.

Page 76
1. that; 2. whom; 3. whomever; 4. Whichever; 5. Whoever; 6. whose; 7. which; 8. who; 9. where; 10. when; 11. why; 12. when

Page 77
1. was writing, am writing, will be writing; 2. was swimming; am swimming; will be swimming; 3. was reading; am reading; will be reading; 4. was playing; am playing; will be playing; 5. was eating; am eating; will be eating; 6. was sitting; am sitting; will be sitting; 7. am playing; 8. will be playing; 9. was playing; 10. could; 11. might; 12. must; 13. shall; 14. would

Page 78
1–5. Answers will vary but must be complete sentences with complete subjects and predicates. 6. (boxed) The gentle manatee (circled) lives in shallow water. 7. (underlined) sometimes called sea cows; Answers will vary. 8. (boxed) Most West Indian manatees (circled) live in Florida. 9. (boxed) They (circled) look for food at the water's surface.
10. (underlined) A resting manatee; Answers will vary.

Answer Key

11. (boxed) The average adult manatee (circled) is three meters (9.8 feet) long. 12. (boxed) Manatees (circled) eat all types of plants.

Page 79
1. big, black; 2. delicious, chocolate; 3. six, empty; 4. long, green; 5. pretty, new; 6. between the cracks; 7. for my lunch; 8. on the steps; 9. from a nearby college; 10. about my behavior; 11. It's, its; 12. by, buy; 13. hare, hair; 14. to, too, two; 15. there, their, they're

Page 80
1. "Can we please stay for 10 more minutes?" the children asked. 2. "I knew about the surprise party all along," Jonah admitted. 3. "That was a really silly joke," Alyssa giggled. 4. "I think I have a cold, so don't get too close," Maggie warned. 5. "Shh, she might hear us," Liz whispered. 6. "I didn't mean to do it," the coach cheered. 8. "First, line up all the numbers, and then add them," the teacher explained. 9. "The water in the pool is chilly today," the lifeguard warned. 10. "Stir the ingredients well," the cooking instructor suggested.

Page 81
1. "I thought about taking a bus, but I finally decided to take an airplane," Emily said. 2. "I am not sure," Tony sighed. "I just can't remember where I left my keys." 3. "The treasure is hidden in the forest," the prince whispered. 4. "Did you see where Melinda went?" Tyler asked. "I want to invite her over for lunch." 5. Sue asked, "Do you know how to grow an herb garden?" 6. "I want to learn to play the cello," Maria said. "Will you teach me?" 7. "Jelly beans are my favorite!" Daniel shouted. "I love the cherry-flavored ones."

Page 82
world, nights, Krusades, liturature, catolog, yung, write, section, for, beautiful, desined, staned.
1. world; 2. knights; 3. Crusades; 4. literature; 5 catalog; 6. young; 7. right; 8. section; 9. four; 10. beautiful; 11. designed; 12. stained

Page 83
1–5. Answers will vary but should convey the appropriate emotion. 6. S, P; 7. P, S; 8. S, P; 9. P, S, 10. S, P

Page 84
1. ?; 2. ?; 3. ?; 4. !; 5. !; 6. ?; 7. !; 8. ?; 9. You will not believe this! 10. What are you talking about? 11. Wow! A snail has teeth on its tongue! 12. Goodness! There are thousands of little teeth!

Page 85
Answers will vary but should resemble: 1. highly ranked; 2. worthy of respect; 3. beat, conquered; 4. power, authority; 5. like a king; 6. occupied a place; 7. stories that have been passed down

Page 86
1–10. Answers will vary

Page 87
Answers will vary but may include 1. easy to do; 2. speechless, can't find the right words; 3. old; far along in life; 4. go to bed; 5. ready to listen; 6–8. Answers will vary.

Page 88
1. M; 2. S; 3. S; 4. M; 5. S; 6–7. Answers will vary but must include either a metaphor or a simile. 8. B; 9. A; 10. A; 11. B; 12. B

Page 89
1. old; 2. hot; 3. dirty; 4. win; 5. catch; 6. fast; 7. humble; 8. sloppy; 9. pretty; 10. quiet; 11. small; 12. intelligent; 13. old; 14. party; 15. tired; 16. hard

Page 90
1–5. Answers will vary.

Notes

Notes